The Translator's Visibility

Literatures, Cultures, Translation

Literatures, Cultures, Translation presents books that engage central issues in translation studies such as history, politics, and gender in and of literary translation, as well as books that open new avenues for study. Volumes in the series follow two main strands of inquiry: one strand brings a wider context to translation through an interdisciplinary interrogation, while the other hones in on the history and politics of the translation of seminal works in literary and intellectual history.

Series Editors
Brian James Baer, Kent State University, USA
Michelle Woods, The State University of New York, New Paltz, USA

Editorial Board
Paul Bandia, Professeur titulaire, Concordia University, Canada, and Senior Fellow, the W.E.B. Du Bois Institute for African American Research, Harvard University, USA
Susan Bassnett, Professor of Comparative Literature, Warwick University, UK.
Leo Tak-hung Chan, Lingnan University, Hong Kong, China
Michael Cronin, Dublin City University, Republic of Ireland
Edwin Gentzler, University of Massachusetts Amherst, USA
Carol Maier, Kent State University, USA
Denise Merkle, Moncton University, Canada
Michaela Wolf, University of Graz, Austria

Volumes in the Series
Translation and the Making of Modern Russian Literature
Brian James Baer
Interpreting in Nazi Concentration Camps
Edited by Michaela Wolf
Exorcising Translation: Towards an Intercivilizational Turn
Douglas Robinson

Literary Translation and the Making of Originals
Karen Emmerich
The Translator on Stage
Geraldine Brodie
Transgender, Translation, Translingual Address
Douglas Robinson
Western Theory in East Asian Contexts: Translation and Translingual Writing
Leo Tak-hung Chan
The Translator's Visibility: Scenes from Contemporary Latin American Fiction
Heather Cleary
The Relocation of Culture: Translations, Migrations, Borders
(forthcoming)
Simona Bertacco and Nicoletta Vallorani

The Translator's Visibility

Scenes from Contemporary Latin American Fiction

Heather Cleary

BLOOMSBURY ACADEMIC
NEW YORK • LONDON • OXFORD • NEW DELHI • SYDNEY

BLOOMSBURY ACADEMIC
Bloomsbury Publishing Inc
1385 Broadway, New York, NY 10018, USA
50 Bedford Square, London, WC1B 3DP, UK

BLOOMSBURY, BLOOMSBURY ACADEMIC and the Diana logo
are trademarks of Bloomsbury Publishing Plc

First published in the United States of America 2021
This paperback edition published 2022

Copyright © Heather Cleary, 2021

For legal purposes the Acknowledgments on p. 157–159 constitute
an extension of this copyright page.

Cover design by Daniel Benneworth-Gray
Cover image: *Script, 1996-2002* © Jan Hendrix

All rights reserved. No part of this publication may be reproduced or transmitted in any form or by any means, electronic or mechanical, including photocopying, recording, or any information storage or retrieval system, without prior permission in writing from the publishers.

Bloomsbury Publishing Inc does not have any control over, or responsibility for, any third-party websites referred to or in this book. All internet addresses given in this book were correct at the time of going to press. The author and publisher regret any inconvenience caused if addresses have changed or sites have ceased to exist, but can accept no responsibility for any such changes.

Whilst every effort has been made to locate copyright holders the publishers would be grateful to hear from any person(s) not here acknowledged.

Library of Congress Cataloging-in-Publication Data
Names: Cleary, Heather, author.
Title: The translator's visibility : scenes from contemporary Latin American fiction / Heather Cleary.
Description: New York : Bloomsbury Academic, 2021. | Series: Literatures, cultures, translation | Includes bibliographical references and index. | Summary: "At the juncture of translation theory and literary criticism, The Translator's Visibility reveals the radical notion of creativity behind the motif of translation in contemporary Latin American fiction, and explores the cultural and political implications of the unique relationship this gesture establishes between language and power"–Provided by publisher.
Identifiers: LCCN 2020034872 | ISBN 9781501353697 (hardback) | ISBN 9781501353703 (epub) | ISBN 9781501353710 (pdf) | ISBN 9781501373459 (paperback)
Subjects: LCSH: Latin American fiction–20th century–History and criticism. | Latin American fiction–21st century–History and criticism. | Translators in literature. | Translating and interpreting in literature.
Classification: LCC PQ7082.N7 T676 2021 | DDC 863/.6098–dc23
LC record available at https://lccn.loc.gov/2020034872

ISBN:	HB:	978-1-5013-5369-7
	PB:	978-1-5013-7345-9
	ePDF:	978-1-5013-5371-0
	eBook:	978-1-5013-5370-3

Typeset by Integra Software Services Pvt. Ltd

To find out more about our authors and books visit www.bloomsbury.com
and sign up for our newsletters.

Contents

Introduction: Against Propriety		1
I. A Tradition of Translation		2
II. The Translator's Visibility		16
1	Monsters and Parricides	23
	I. Tea for One	29
	II. In the Name of the Father	35
	III. Of Bastards and Clones	40
2	Foreign Correspondence	55
	I. A Few Notes on (Un)Translation	59
	II. Fragments of a Vessel	64
	III. The Problem with False Friends	70
	IV. The Problem with True Friends	74
	V. Best Enemies	83
3	Writing in the Margins	87
	I. On the (Foot-)Printed Page	93
	II. The Hermeneutic (Com-)Motion	100
	III. A Re-writer on the Edge	110
	IV. Playing Along	115
4	Writing off the Map	121
	I. Carpet and Fringe	129
	II. Quite a View You've Got Here	134
	III. Into the Woods	143
Coda: Reading for Distance		151
Acknowledgments		157
Bibliography		160
Index		181

Introduction: Against Propriety

A promising young translator crumples into a weeping ball on the floor of a crowded Buenos Aires theater while interpreting for Derrida, whom he accuses of inventing the word "valise." A murder is committed to appease a literary idol angered by a shoddy rendering of his work. A translator who moonlights as a mad scientist sets out to clone a genius and ends up unleashing unimaginable terrors on a coastal city in Venezuela. A young woman disrupts the modernist canon with forged translations attributed to a Mexican poet.

On the eve of the twenty-first century, as discussions of globalization hit a fever pitch and theories of world literature returned with a late capitalist spin, a remarkable proliferation began in Latin America of novels that feature translation as a principal element.[1] *The Translator's Visibility: Scenes from Contemporary Latin American Fiction* explores what it means, in the specific context of

---

[1] Though globalization is often discussed as the monolithic spread of hegemonic cultural products and norms, it is not a homogeneous phenomenon. In Latin America, the early 1990s saw a surge of foreign investments and privatizations; these neoliberal policies were ostensibly aimed at establishing political alliances and accessing international credit markets. This is the time of the North American Free Trade Agreement (NAFTA) and the Argentine Convertibility Plan, to name but two examples, which had—and continue to have—devastating effects that include rampant femicides (especially at, but not limited to, the border between Mexico and the United States), economic crises, and the unchecked exploitation of human and natural resources. The novels studied in the pages that follow were written in the aftermath of these failed policies. While these issues inform my approach throughout, they are treated most explicitly in Chapters 2 and 4. For more, see Sayak Valencia's *Capitalismo Gore* (2010) [translated into English as *Gore Capitalism* by J. D. Pluecker in 2018], Rénique 2005, and Lewkowicz 2015; for specific reflections on the publishing industry in Argentina in the early 2000s, see Allen 2007 (53–8).

Latin American literature, to center a work of fiction on a translator. I contend that these recent novels, drawing on Latin America's long tradition of critical and creative engagement with translation, explicitly mobilize major tropes of translation theory to challenge notions of intellectual property and propriety. They address the asymmetries of discursive authority, the conditions under which cultural goods circulate, and the persistent dichotomy between the so-called "creative" traditions of the metropolis and derivative "translating" cultures at the periphery. By foregrounding translation in their fiction, the writers examined in these pages construct a dynamic, reciprocal model of creativity grounded in reference and appropriation over and against that of the sacrosanct author. These novels show how translation not only serves to renew national literatures through an exchange of ideas and forms but also, when rendered visible, can help us reimagine the terms according to which those exchanges take place.

Ultimately, this is a book about language and power: not the ways in which power wields language, but rather the ways in which language can be used to unseat power. Three foundational narratives, chosen from many, sketch the contours of what I describe above as the tradition of translation in Latin America, understood as the conscious and sustained mobilization of the practice coupled with a reflection upon its political and cultural implications.[2]

I. A Tradition of Translation

In 1519, a young woman is given as tribute to Hernán Cortés, along with other gifts including chickens, corn, and gold. Her name is

---

[2] One of the best sources on these antecedents is Nora Catelli and Marietta Gargatagli's expansive compilation, *El tabaco que fumaba Plinio. Escenas de la traducción en España y América* (1998) [The tobacco Pliny smoked: scenes of translation in Spain and America].

Malinalli Tenepal, that is, until the Spaniards christen her as Marina. Other names follow: Malintzin and la Malinche, a designation that marks her as property, as the woman of her master.[3] This is not the first time she has been given away: after the death of her father, a cacique in the region now known as Veracruz, Malinalli was sold off as a slave and became the property of a cacique in Potonchán, Tabasco. Raised speaking Nahuatl, she learns Chontal Maya in this new land. When she is subsequently offered to Cortés after the fall of Pontochán, she is called upon to translate between these two languages; Gerónimo de Aguilar, a Spanish friar able to speak Maya, would then convey her words to Cortés. Malintzin's role as interpreter brings with it another name: *la lengua* or "the tongue," which reduces her metonymically to her function within the machinery of the conquest. Later, she will become "la Chingada," an allusion to both the sexual violence visited upon her by the Spaniards and the impossible position she was forced to occupy under their rule (Alarcón 1989: 61). Malintzin was both a vehicle of the conquest and its victim, and because she left no written record of her own, her body and legacy remain contested ideological property. She has been described as the ultimate traitor, a victim of colonial violence, the monstrous double of the Virgin of Guadalupe, and the harbinger of a society marked by *mestizaje*; once labeled "the whore of Cortés" (Alarcón 1989: 58), she

---

[3] Pilar Godayol, with reference to the writings of Bernal Díaz del Castillo, explains la Malinche's multiple names:

> At her baptism, the priest gave her the name of Marina ... Marina was altered into Malina: the Spanish "r" does not exist in the Nahautl alphabet ... Malina became Malintzin: the suffix "-tzin" in Nahautl indicates respect. Cortés was known as Malintzin-é but the Spaniards replaced the "tzin-é" with the Spanish "che" and the result was Malinche. So Cortés was named Malinche, which according to Díaz del Castillo means "the captain of Marina" ... La Malinche means "the wife of the captain."
>
> (2012: 65)

According to this account, even the name Malintzin, which recovers a Nahuatl form of respect, is based on the name assigned to her by the oppressor according to a religious practice that had also been foisted upon her. La Malinche means, literally, that she is the wife of the man who is captain (master) of the woman she came to be named. La Chingada, the name that followed much later, translates as "the fucked woman," both literally and figuratively.

has more recently been claimed as an emblem of Chicana feminism and as the ultimate cultural mediator.[4] The violent encounter of conquest and colonization also provided Brazil with its central figure for conceiving of translation as a motor of culture and politics: that of the cannibal, resemanticized in the 1920s by Brazilian modernists who mobilized the figure as a means not only to criticize neocolonial domination, but also to destabilize the opposition between originality and derivation along the way.[5] A key aspect of the movement was the way it recast the cannibal as a cultural agent with the power to selectively digest, and in doing so, reconstitute, the material and larger tradition he devours. Epitomizing this gesture, Oswald de Andrade's "Manifesto Antropófago" [Cannibalist Manifesto] was published in May of 1928 in the first issue—or "dentition," as the editors called it—of the *Revista de Antropofagia*. Eschewing the Gregorian calendar entirely, Andrade signs his manifesto "In Piratininga, in the 374th Year of the Swallowing of Bishop Sardinha" (1991: 44).[6] In so doing, he replaces a concept of history centered on the Metropolis, its ideology, and its colonial expansion with one centered on autochthonous culture and its resistance to (through its consumption of) that history. Even more subversive is the fact that this manifesto inserts itself within the hegemonic discourse. Rather than presenting a radical break with European models, Andrade's project is one of ingesting and digesting those inherited ideas in the process of creating a new work. The Manifesto's third statement, its most quoted, "Tupi or not tupi,

---

[4] The opposition between the Virgin of Guadalupe and la Malinche (la Chingada) as the two mothers of Mexico—one virginal, one the victim of rape—is presented by Octavio Paz in *El laberinto de la soledad* (1950) [*The Labyrinth of Solitude* trans. Lysander Kemp 1961]. For more on Malintzin, see Thomas 1993 (170–3) and Townsend 2006; for contemporary approaches to this mythic figure, see Alarcón 1989, Godayol 2012, and, in Spanish, Glantz 1992 and 1994.

[5] This appropriation of the figure of the cannibal begins at the famous 1922 Semana de Arte Moderna in São Paolo and was taken up by both Mário and Oswald de Andrade (no relation), as well as the visual artists Anita Malfatti and Tarsila do Amaral (whose 1928 canvas "Abaporu" would become an iconic image of the Cannibalist movement).

[6] As legend has it, Pedro Fernandes Sardinha was shipwrecked off the coast of Alagoas in 1556, two weeks after resigning his post, and was eaten by one of the tribes that made up the Tupi peoples.

that is the question" (1991: 38)—presented in English in the original Portuguese text—is a key example of this negotiation of the foreign and the local: at once violently depositing Hamlet on the inhospitable shores of the cannibal and retroactively inserting the anthropophagus into the Shakespearean literary system, Andrade renders unstable this pillar of the Western canon and relativizes its cultural and discursive authority.[7]

The figure of the cannibal is taken up again in the second half of the twentieth century, when the concrete poet Haroldo de Campos developed both a theory and a practice of "transcriação" or "transcreation," presented in a 1981 article titled "Da razão antropofágica: A Europa sob o signo da devoração" ["The Rule of Anthropophagy: Europe under the Sign of Devoration"]. Whereas the modernist version of cannibalism emphasized the *transformative* power of the consuming culture over that of the culture consumed (the material that was not "spit out" as noxious would be transformed by its incorporation in the new system), Haroldo de Campos insists on a state of coexistence and stresses the creative intervention of writing *through* another work. In the introduction to their *Traduzir & Trovar* (1968) [*Translate & Versify*], Haroldo and his brother Augusto de Campos write "Traduzir & Trovar são dois aspectos da mesma realidade. Trovar quer dizer achar, quer dizer inventar. Traduzir é reinventar" (3) [To translate and to compose verse are two aspects of the same reality. To compose is to think, to invent. To translate is to reinvent]. Around the same time, Augusto de Campos developed the complementary idea of *Intradução*, a portmanteau that suggests both "un-translation," in the sense of the

---

[7] Haroldo de Campos invokes the concept of *parody* in his description of Oswald de Andrade's literary legacy. Parody, he reminds us, is etymologically grounded in the "parallel canto" (pará + ôidê): as such it is not derivative, but rather represents a creative operation that occurs *beside* another work, engaging it in a dialogue that defines both. The line from the Manifesto, cited above, of "Tupi or not tupi, that is the question" is exemplary of this kind of parody: the appropriation of Shakespeare's text is only the first movement in a process that, per the quotation above, re-imagines the canonical work in a local context. See de Campos's prologue to *Oswald de Andrade: Obra escogida* (Caracas: Biblioteca Ayacucho, 1979).

negation of translation in its more limiting definition, and "intraduction" or movement within, the internalization and adaptation of the text (1995: np).

Translation and violence—both symbolic and physical—are also inextricably intertwined in the work of the Argentinean intellectual and politician Domingo Faustino Sarmiento, whose energies in the process of national consolidation were dedicated to translating prolifically and forming the nascent republic in the image of Europe and North America. Sarmiento is known for many things, chief among them for being president of Argentina from 1868 to 1874, and for the foundational text *Facundo: civilización y barbarie* (1845), translated most recently into English by Kathleen Ross as *Facundo: Civilization and Barbarism* in 2003, a scathing indictment of the dictator Juan Manuel de Rosas written while Sarmiento was in exile in Chile.[8] Described by Ricardo Piglia as "the first page of Argentine literature" (1994: 131), the text is structured around the diametrical opposition between "civilization" and "barbarism," the former being associated with Northern Europe, North America, and the urban sphere, while the latter is tied to Spain, Asia, the countryside, and Sarmiento's political enemies.

In what could be called the work's primal scene, Sarmiento describes his final act of rebellion before fleeing his homeland. "A fines del año 1840," he writes, "salía yo de mi patria desterrado por lástima, estropeado, lleno de cardenales, puntazos y golpes ... bajo las Armas de la Patria que en días más alegres había pintado en una sala, escribí con carbón estas palabras: *On ne tue point les idées*" (1977: xiv) [Toward the end of 1840 I was leaving my homeland, pitifully exiled, broken,

---

[8] In *Mi defensa* (1843) [My defense] and *Recuerdos de provincia* (1850) [Memories of a provincial past], Sarmiento places translation at the heart of both his writings and his politics. Esther Allen offers a fascinating account of the first translation into English of the *Facundo* in 1868 by Mary (Mrs. Horace) Mann in "The Will to Translate," while the edited volume *Sarmiento, Author of a Nation* (1994) includes a variety of essays relevant to the present discussion; see also Diana Sorensen's *Facundo and the Construction of Argentine Culture* (1996) and Carlos J. Alonso's exploration of the political implications of Sarmiento's rhetorical idiosyncrasies in "Reading Sarmiento: Once More, with Passion" (1994).

covered with bruises, kicks, and blows ... beneath a national coat of arms that in happier days I had painted in a room, I wrote these words with charcoal: *On ne tue point les idées* (2003: 30)]. Emphasizing the vast divide between his "civilized" command of French and the barbarism that surrounds him, Sarmiento goes on to assert that Rosas's government, "mandó una comisión encargada de descifrar el jeroglífico, que se decía contener desahogos innobles, insultos y amenazas. Oída la traducción, 'y bien! – dijeron – ¿qué significa esto?'" (1977: xiv) [sent a commission in charge of deciphering the hieroglyph, which was said to contain base venting, insults, and threats. Upon hearing the translation, "So!" they said, "what does this mean?" (2003: 30)]. Even more notable than the delight with which Sarmiento pens this scene is translation's place within it. His gesture of refusing translation, of writing the words in their "original" French, is intuitive enough: he wants to underscore the ignorance of his adversaries. Curiously, though, it is not the foreign phrase itself that gives the soldiers trouble—in this account, someone is apparently able to supply a translation—but rather its meaning.[9]

So, what *does* it mean? The same French phrase appears just a few lines earlier as an epigraph: if this is a primal scene, it is also one marked by a repetition compulsion. There, it is attributed to Fortoul and translated beneath as "A los hombres se degüella, a las ideas no" [Men can have their throats cut, but ideas can't]; Sarmiento's translation presents two—easily perceptible—alterations, adding in the body of a man and a more vivid image of death than appears in the French. It is his own persecuted body that he inserts, and in so doing he joins it to the body of his beloved nation, wracked by the barbarism of Rojas. But his textual machinations don't end there. "We must not forget," Piglia writes, "that his motto is a quotation: a sentence from Diderot which

---

[9] This "oída la traducción" seems to present two possibilities: either Sarmiento is unaware that his narration of the event undermines his own gesture of establishing difference according to an alignment with the civilized metropolis by making the phrase linguistically accessible to the horde, or he is describing the French itself as a translation, unintentionally distancing himself from that with which he seeks to identify.

Sarmiento misquotes and attributes to Fortoul, thus opening up a line of equivocal references, false quotations, and apocryphal erudition which is a sign of Argentine culture at least up to the time of Borges" (1994: 132).[10] And so it is. Nearly a century after Sarmiento placed literary and institutional translation at the heart of his project of national development, Jorge Luis Borges posited the creative potential of textual appropriation and manipulation, reimagining the position of Latin America on the global cultural stage during a period of intense intellectual and translational activity in Argentina.[11] A prolific translator in his own right—his first translation, of Oscar Wilde's "The Happy Prince," was published before he was ten, followed by the writings of Joyce, Faulkner, Poe, Chesterton, and many others—Borges frequently engaged the practice in his fiction and essays, famously asserting in, "Las versiones homéricas" (1932) ["The Homeric Versions"], that no problem "is as consubstantial to literature and its modest mystery as the one posed by translation" (2000: 69).[12] The essay, one of his best

---

[10] Adding yet another layer to these mistranslations and misattributions, Esther Allen pointed out to me in personal correspondence that "Ricardo Piglia was either mistaken in attributing the phrase 'on ne tue point les idées' to Diderot (or horrified by its actual provenance): 'On ne tire pas de coups de fusil aux idées' is a phrase not from the revolutionary *philosophe* but from the Royalist translator Antoine de Rivaroli, known as Rivarol." For his part, Piglia invokes and expands upon these interrelated practices of translation and textual appropriation in his own work, most vividly in *La ciudad ausente* (1992) [*The Absent City*, translated by Sergio Waisman in 2000]. For more on translation in Piglia's oeuvre, see Sergio Waisman's "Ethics and Aesthetics in North and South" (2001).

[11] A crucial part of this activity was the international literary journal *Sur* [South], directed by Victoria Ocampo, which published its first volume in 1931. Patricia Willson's *La constelación del sur: traductores y traducciones en la literatura argentina del siglo XX* (2004) [The southern constellation: translators and translations in twentieth-century Argentine literature] offers a rich portrait of this moment.

[12] Borges casts a long shadow over pretty much everything written after him (and, like his own character Pierre Menard, many texts that came before him). This entire book could focus on the contemporary echoes of different facets of his principal texts on translation and textual appropriation ("The Homeric Versions" [1932], "The Translators of the 1001 Nights" [1936], and "The Argentine Writer and Tradition" [1951], which will be discussed at length in Chapter 4; among his fiction, there is "Pierre Menard, Author of the Quixote" [1939], which will also be discussed at length, as well as "Tlön, Uqbar, Orbis Tertius" [1940] and "Averroës's Search" [1947], to name just a few), but there are already several scholarly volumes that do an excellent job of that. See especially Waisman 2005 and Kristal 2002.

known, centers on divergent translations of Homer's great epics and the questions these raise with regard to fidelity. Arguing that all are equally faithful and equally unfaithful because all represent a recombination of textual elements that crosses into new territories not only of language but also of time, Borges asserts that to believe a translation is necessarily inferior to the original is to "presuponer que el borrador 9 es obligatoriamente inferior al borrador H—ya que no puede haber sino borradores. El concepto de *texto definitivo* no corresponde sino a la religión o al cansancio" (1997a: 130) [assume that draft nine is necessarily inferior to draft H—for there can only be drafts. The concept of the "definitive text" corresponds only to religion or exhaustion (2000: 69)]. Borges illustrates his rejection of the subordinate status of the translation by presenting his "drafts" as belonging to two entirely different systems of annotation: one alphabetic, the other numerical. In so doing, he asserts that versions cannot be judged by the same criteria, but that each must instead be approached on its own terms, according to its own specificity. The ludic dimension of this model is borne out in Borges's own translational practice, most notably in his fragmentary and highly localized rendering of James Joyce's seminal work of literary modernism, *Ulysses*.[13]

Translation also made frequent appearances in Borges's fiction—most notably in "Pierre Menard, autor del Quijote" (1939) ["Pierre Menard, Author of the Quixote"]. The story is framed as the posthumous defense of a French writer whom the narrator claims has been misrepresented by other critics. After an extensive inventory of Menard's "visible work," which includes several translations and a dizzying array of

---

[13] Borges's translation, published in the January 1925 issue of *Proa*, though recognized for its stylistic fidelity, reproduced only the final lines of Joyce's novel and frequently effaced the geographic specificity of the original by eliding or substituting local references, beginning with the domestion of the author as "Jaime" Joyce (for further reading, see Battistón 2001, Willson 2004, and Waisman 2005). Along similar lines, Efraín Kristal has observed that, in his translation of "The Honour of Israel Gow" by G. K. Chesterton, Borges "took liberties to ensure that the story would conform to his own view that Chesterton's genius lay in his ability to present inexplicable situations that, even once demystified with a prosaic explanation, continue to disconcert" (2002: 69).

philosophical monographs, invectives, and other discursive forms, the narrator goes on to describe Menard's "invisible work," his "admirable ambition" (1999: 91) not to translate the canonical text or even copy it, but instead to "producir unas páginas que coincidieran—palabra por palabra y línea por línea—con las de Miguel de Cervantes" (2011: 111) [produce a number of pages which coincided—word for word and line for line—with those of Miguel de Cervantes (1999: 91)]. Though the story has been described as one of the most acute commentaries ever offered about translation, it is important to point out that Menard's endeavor is not one, at least not in the interlingual sense—its radical gesture resides in the retroactive effect that Menard's project has on the work it engages.[14] As we will see in greater detail in Chapter 4, Menard does not produce an updated version that supplants the original: simply by shifting the attribution of the words on the page, he actually reconstitutes Cervantes's text. In so doing, he establishes a mode of reading that dismantles the fixity of the author sign and, with it, the idea that a work can "belong" to its author, whoever that might be.

The geopolitical resonances of this challenge to textual property and propriety are further explored in an address given in 1951 and later published as "El escritor argentino y la tradición" ["The Argentine Writer and Tradition"]. In his remarks, Borges argues that so-called peripheral cultures are in a uniquely privileged position from which to innovate, precisely because the writer at the margin is able to engage the canonical works of the metropolis without the same "superstitions" that limit the members of those traditions. "Creo que nuestra tradición," he writes, "es toda la cultura occidental ... que los argentinos, los sudamericanos en general ... podemos manejar todos los temas europeos, manejarlos sin supersticiones, con una irreverencia que puede tener, y ya tiene, consecuencias afortunadas" (1997a: 200–1) [I believe that our tradition is the whole of Western culture ... that Argentines, and South Americans in general ... can take on all the European subjects, take

---

[14] The remark about the story as an acute commentary on translation is from George Steiner's *After Babel* (1975: 73).

them on without superstition and with an irreverence than can have, and already has had, fortunate consequences (2000: 426)]. Rather than presenting a disadvantage, for Borges the margin becomes a privileged site from which to exercise uninhibited textual manipulation and reject the constraints of intellectual propriety.[15]

The examples cited above, which represent only a small cross-section of a broad and varied phenomenon, give a sense of the extent to which translation has long played a pivotal role in Latin American culture and politics. They are also meant to underscore the intrinsically political nature of translation: whether in the service of a colonial, neocolonial, or anti-neocolonial project, translation is never neutral.[16] Nor are its agents: as an individual operating at a specific set of subjective coordinates, the translator is both the vehicle that allows for the transfer of information across languages and cultures, and a point of friction within that transfer. As Silviano Santiago asserts in *The Space In-Between*:

> The major contribution of Latin America to Western culture is to be found in its systematic destruction of the concepts of *unity* and *purity*: these two concepts lose the precise contours of their meaning, they lose their crushing weight, their sign of cultural superiority ... Latin America establishes its place on the map of Western civilization by actively and destructively diverting the European norm and resignifying preestablished and immutable elements that were exported to the New World by the Europeans.
>
> (2001: 30)

Translation is presented here an essential lever in the negotiation of global relations of discursive authority and, by extension, of hegemonic

---

[15] The title of Sergio Waisman's excellent 2005 study, *Borges and Translation: The Irreverence of the Periphery*, is derived from this assertion.
[16] I borrow the term anti-neocolonial from Don Mee Choi's recent *Translation is a Mode = Translation is an Anti-neocolonial Mode* (2020). "For me," Choi writes, "Benjamin's 'Translation is a mode' must be jointed with 'Translation is an anti-neocolonial mode.' I must speak as a twin ... I want to make impossible connections between the Korean and the English, for they are misaligned by neocolonial war, militarism, and neoliberal economy" (3–5).

ideologies. The fact that social and cultural institutions determine what is to be translated and how it is to be rendered has been theorized in numerous cultural contexts, but in Latin America from very early on the interaction between political and cultural production is of a highly symbiotic nature: the translations of the colonial period and the first years after independence engender the very institutions that foster and define the scope of future translations, while in the decades and centuries that follow, the practice is engaged not only on a practical, but also a thematic or metaphorical level as an anti-neocolonial response to the hierarchies of global cultural relations.

These dynamics of exchange and consecration have played a central role in the literary production of the region, as well. As Else Ribeiro Pires Vieira observes, "The question of the translator's visibility, as far back as Modernism, takes on very clear contours in Latin America," decolonizing, in the process, "two spaces traditionally deemed marginal: translation itself and a peripheral culture" (1998: 173). This visibility became notable as a consolidated tendency during the 1960s and 1970s, when the writers of the Boom developed a markedly (market-ly) international focus and brought translation to the fore, not only by creating a sudden demand for translations from the Spanish into the languages of the global publishing industry, but also because the writers of this loosely associated "generation" often highlighted the process of interlinguistic transfer on a thematic level. Gabriel García Márquez's *Cien años de soledad* (1967) [translated into English by Gregory Rabassa as *One Hundred Years of Solitude* in 1970] is framed, in the tradition of the *Quixote*, as a translation in and of itself; Julio Cortázar, too, centers the practice in many novels and short stories— not surprising, given the years he spent working as a translator; one of the earliest among these, "Carta a una señorita en París" (1951) ["Letter to a Young Lady in Paris"] will be discussed in the next chapter. Mario Vargas Llosa's *El hablador* (1987) [*The Storyteller* trans. Helen Lane 1989] is a meditation on cultural translation in the Amazon; the Nobel laureate and former presidential candidate would revisit the theme of translation in a more metropolitan context in his *Travesuras de la niña mala* (2006) [*The Bad Girl* trans. Edith Grossman 2008], whose translator protagonist suffers perennially from his love of a Flaubertian femme fatale.

This list, however, pales in comparison to the novels featuring translators that have been published in Latin America since the mid-1990s. To name but a few: in Argentina, Marcelo Cohen's *El testamento de O'Jaral* [The testament of O'Jaral] and Graciela Safranchik's *El cangrejo* [The crab] were published in 1995, followed in 1998 by three aptly titled novels with translator protagonists—Salvador Benesdra's *El traductor* [The translator], Pablo De Santis's *La traducción* [The translation], and Néstor Ponce's *El intérprete* [The interpreter].[17] In 2000, the Brazilian humorist Luis Fernando Verissimo published the metafictional mystery *Borges e os orangutangos eternos* [*Borges and the Eternal Orangutans* trans. Margaret Jull Costa 2004], while in 2003 his compatriot Francisco "Chico" Buarque came out with *Budapeste* [*Budapest* trans. Alison Entrekin 2005]. These works were followed by Pedro Mairal's *El año del desierto* (2005) [The year of the desert], Mario Vargas Llosa's aforementioned *Las travesuras de la niña mala* (2006), Mariano Siskind's *Histora del Abasto* (2007) [The (hi)story of el Abasto], Andrés Neuman's *El viajero del siglo* (2009) [*Traveler of the Century* trans. Nick Caistor and Lorenza García 2013], Valeria Luiselli's *Los ingrávidos* (2011) [*Faces in the Crowd* trans. Christina MacSweeney 2014], and Cristina Rivera Garza's *El mal de la taiga* (2012) [*The Taiga Syndrome* trans. Suzanne Jill Levine and Aviva Kana 2018]. Among the many writers who have mobilized translation in their fiction, three stand out for the consistency with which they return to the theme: César Aira (*El congreso de literatura*, 1999 [*The Literary Conference* trans. Katherine Silver 2010]; *El juego de los mundos*, 2000 [The game of worlds]; *La Princesa Primavera*, 2003 [Princess Springtime]), Mario Bellatin (*El jardín de la señora Murakami*, 2000 [*Mrs. Murakami's Garden* trans. Heather Cleary 2020]; *Shiki Nagaoka: una nariz de*

---

[17] Benesdra's novel was a finalist for the Planeta Prize in 1995; it did not win, nor did the novel see publication until two years after the author's death.

ficción, 2000 [*Shiki Nagaoka: A Nose for Fiction* trans. David Shook 2012], and Alan Pauls (*El pasado*, 2003 [*The Past* trans. Nick Caistor 2007]; *Historia del pelo*, 2010 [A (hi)story of hair]). This list is by no means exhaustive.

Understanding this surge in representations of the translator in contemporary Latin American fiction involves recognizing the growing focus on the practice in discussions of cultural exchange in the context of globalization. Lisa Bradford, in her introduction to *Traducción como cultura* (1997) [Translation as culture], insists that the study of translation has expanded so dramatically in the age of globalization, "porque al aprehender la dinámica de la transferencia cultural, se revela significante información respecto de la formación de una identidad cultural y de la práctica de representación a través de la materialización lingüística de lo que es considerado como *propio* u otro" (13, my italics) [because by grasping the dynamics of cultural transfer, one reveals significant information regarding the formation of cultural identity and the practice of representation through the linguistic materialization of what is considered one's own, and what is considered Other]. Key here is the idea that translation can serve as a framework for understanding broad intercultural processes, that cultural identity is formed *through* translational practices (though we also know that what is translated and how it is rendered is conditioned by cultural—and institutional—identity, as well).

I want to linger for a moment on Bradford's use of the term *propio*. *Propio*, like the English "proper," denotes ownership or belonging while also indicating suitability or conformity; by extension, *propiedad* is the linguistic intersection of ownership and correctness at the heart of the capitalist social contract: it is both the state of being proper and the thing that is owned. In modern-day English usage, the term is split as "property" and "propriety" (a distinction not registered before the eighteenth century—around the same time the Statute of Anne [1710] laid the groundwork of copyright law), but I hope you'll hear the echoes of this polysemy as we read the resistance mounted by these contemporary novels to the notion and structures of *propiedad intelectual*—intellectual property in the sense of copyright, which at once depends on and proliferates the notion of the Author as creator and sole owner of a text, and intellectual propriety, in the sense of what one can and cannot do according to a given set of aesthetic, ethical, or social norms. In this way, the foregrounding of translation challenges not only the structures of legitimation whereby discursive authority is conferred, but also the material conditions under which cultural goods circulate globally. As Jacques Lezra points out:

> It is no secret that the group of phenomena that we call "globalization" today takes shape around the differential flow of people, labor, commodities and capital among different regions ... "Translation," the conveying of information between natural languages, is a political concept in this sense: it is at the same time one of the instruments that make possible certain flows, and it is itself what one might call a second-order commodity-practice whose value is established in relation to the flow of capital and of first-order, material commodities.
>
> (2012: 2)

At the same time translators, the "literary proletariat" (Apter 2006: xi), facilitate the flows of global cultural exchange, they are also very much located within that system—albeit at a remove or on a secondary tier, as several of the contemporary writers presented in this study observe. As noted above, translators also challenge the assumption of smooth interlinguistic transfer due to their geographic and cultural situatedness. The translator is thus the nexus of the local and the global, of creativity and derivation, of independence and subjugation—as well as a sign of the cultural and discursive hierarchies through which these categories are mobilized. Ultimately, if the translator-as-practitioner is subject to both the vertical and horizontal structures that comprise the dynamics of global cultural exchange, the translator-as-protagonist offers a means of commenting upon and even subverting these structures from within the text, positing alternative models of creativity grounded in iteration and play rather than chafingly proper notions of author and authoritative original.

II. The Translator's Visibility

The title of this book, a nod to Lawrence Venuti's seminal work *The Translator's Invisibility* (1995), underscores the political dimension of my research. For Venuti, the attempt to conceal the translator's intervention in the process of textual transfer by valorizing above all a translation's "fluency" masks and thereby naturalizes "the numerous conditions under which the translation is made" (1)—conditions that include biases which determine not only what works are translated, but also how these are presented within the target language system. The fact that a translation's quality should be assessed in terms of its ability to be absorbed by the literature of the target language "points to the violence that resides in the very purpose and activity of translation: the reconstitution of the foreign text in accordance with values, beliefs and representations that preexist it in the target language, always configured in hierarchies of dominance and marginality, always determining the production, circulation, and reception of texts" (18).[18] As such, the culturally prescribed invisibility of the translator facilitates the naturalization of dominant ideologies, catering to and perpetuating the preconceptions and predilections of the target system. The *mise en scène* of translation in these contemporary Latin American fictions, then, performs the opposite function, calling attention to the hierarchies and vested interests that subtend this process and, through their denaturalization, opens up a space for alternate intercultural dynamics.

The book's secondary title operates along similar lines by suggesting two interrelated meanings of the word "scene." The first, and most

---

[18] That same year, Jean Delisle and Judith Woodsworth edited a volume of essays titled *Translators Through History* (1995), which sought to counteract the translator's invisibility by reflecting on the many ways these cultural agents have been central in developing national literatures and languages, in disseminating religious beliefs and cultural values, and more. Contributors included Sherry Simon, André Lefevere, and Myriam Salama-Carr. These works were preceded by an enactment of this visibility: Suzanne Jill Levine's indispensable glimpse into the complexities of literary translation, *The Subversive Scribe* (1991).

literal, is that of a scene in a narrative or, just as aptly, a play: there is an element of performance to this metafictional conceit, according to which the mechanisms of international publishing are laid bare (not to mention the fact that many of these translator protagonists are self-referential, their authors also moonlighting as translators). The second valence understands the word "scene" as the locus of spatial-subjective situatedness described by Tejaswini Niranjana in *Siting Translation* (1992). Though this spatial framework comes into play particularly in Chapters 3 and 4, it informs the project as a whole—not only in the interrogation of Eurocentric models of cultural authority, but also in the specificity of the publishing landscape in Latin America, as it relates to the multinational media conglomerates that determine the lion's share of what is published throughout the region, and how (or whether) these works make it into the hands of readers.

Though this volume occupies a relatively uncharted space within translation studies—a monograph in English on contemporary novels from Latin America that feature translators as protagonists—it builds on the work of many scholars in the field. Among these are edited volumes that explore the political dimensions of translation, such as Maria Tymockzo and Edwin Gentzler's *Translation and Power* (2002), Sandra Bermann and Michael Wood's *Nation, Language, and the Ethics of Translation* (2005), Myriam Salama-Carr's *Translating and Interpreting Conflict* (2007), and Liliana Feierstein and Vera Gerling's *Traducción y poder* (2008) [Translation and power], to name but a few. In recent years, several edited volumes have appeared in English that address the "fictional turn" in translation studies, a term coined by the Brazilian scholar Else Ribeiro Pires Vieira in the 1990s. Several of these anthologies build on discussions held at a series of international "Transfiction" conferences (Vienna, 2011; Tel Aviv, 2013; Montreal, 2015; and Guangdong, 2017), including Klaus Kaindl and Karlheinz Spitzl's *Transfiction: Research Into the Realities of Translation Fiction* (2014), a special issue of *Translation and Interpreting Studies* (2016), and Judith Woodsworth's *The Fictions of Translation* (2018). *Linguistica Antverpiensia* also dedicated a special issue in 2005, edited by Dirk Delabastita and Rainier Grutman, to fictional representations of translation and multilingualism.

With notable exceptions, much of the scholarship within this fictional turn approaches the literary representation of the translator with an eye to elucidating, corroborating, or debunking inherited notions about the practice and its practitioners. *The Translator's Visibility* does not propose to do any of that, but instead examines the cultural and political implications of foregrounding the translator in fiction produced at a specific set of cultural coordinates (the more visible Latin American literatures of Argentina, Mexico, and Brazil) at a specific moment in time (the turn of the twenty-first century). As scholarly kinship goes, then, this book is most closely related to Martín Gaspar's *La condición traductora* (2014) [The translator's condition], which also discusses the representation of translators in contemporary Latin American fiction, and which analyzes several of the same novels, though with a different—more psychological, or as Gaspar puts it, temperamental— focus. In terms of works available in English, Edwin Gentzler dedicates a chapter of his *Translation and Identity in Latin America* (2007) to the representation of translators in Borges and the Boom. Closest of all is Rosemary Arrojo's recent monograph *Fictional Translators: Rethinking Translation Through Literature* (2018), which includes the readings of Moacyr Scliar and Rodolfo Walsh that consolidated my interest in narratives of translation early on, but which focuses on twentieth-century fictions and employs a different methodological approach.

The novels examined in the pages that follow were selected for the way they engage certain key tropes of translation theory— namely, gendered and biogenetic notions of textual reproduction, untranslatability, and the physical and textual spaces associated with the translator. The first chapter, "Monsters and Parricides," focuses on tropes of translation theory grounded in metaphors of gendered and biogenetic reproduction, such as Lori Chamberlain's gendered metaphorics of translation and Emily Apter's alignment of pseudotranslation and cloning. I read—through Graciela Safranchik's *El cangrejo*, Luis Fernando Verissimo's *Borges e os orangotangos eternos*, and César Aira's *El congreso de literatura*—the ways in which notions of intellectual filiation are transformed in contemporary translation narratives to challenge the idea of derivative cultural production.

In Chapter 2, "Foreign Correspondence," I engage current formulations of untranslatability (exemplified by Barbara Cassin's *Dictionary of Untranslatables*) to assert that identifying certain terms as "untranslatable" falsely presupposes the existence of terms that are unproblematically translatable. To this end, I read Salvador Benesdra's *El traductor*, Alan Pauls's *El pasado*, and Pablo De Santis's *La traducción* through the theoretical writings of Walter Benjamin and Jacques Derrida, constructing an analysis of scenes of translation failure that center on those moments that would appear to present the least resistance to transfer: the transmission of cognates. From here, I propose a *distancing* practice of reading that privileges specificity and complexity over expediency and the imposition of local norms.

While the two chapters described above challenge the strictures of intellectual property and propriety and assert the essential and often radical creativity of translation, the next two chapters—"Writing in the Margins" and "Writing off the Map"—address the persistence of the center/periphery dichotomy in formulations of world literature and outline the ways in which the fictions of the corpus manipulate the physical and textual spaces assigned to translation to subvert the very notion of marginality.

"Writing in the Margins" traces how Mario Bellatin's pseudotranslation *El jardín de la señora Murakami* severs the body of the text from the space of its own footnotes and appendix, placing them at odds; these paratexts eventually absorb the work they comment on, and in so doing, present translation as a form of usurpation and, ultimately, dominance. "Writing off the Map" performs a similar operation on the geographic, rather than textual, spaces associated with the translator as a means of asserting the privileged perspective afforded by the translator's physical (and professional) marginality. Reflecting on spatial conceptions of cultural production formulated by Jorge Luis Borges and Homi Bhabha, I posit that novels like Valeria

Luiselli's *Los ingrávidos*, César Aira's *La Princesa Primavera*, Salvador Benesdra's *El traductor*, Pablo De Santis's *La traducción*, and Cristina Rivera Garza's *El mal de la taiga* set the translator both inside and outside the national designations upon which the uneven distribution of cultural authority depends. Finally, a coda explores strategies for bringing the constellation of questions raised by these texts into the classroom.

Before delving into the first chapter, a brief note. As Karen Emmerich observes in her excellent *Literary Translation and the Making of Originals* (2017), translation is still marginalized as intellectual labor within academia, a situation that forces translators who are also academics to "check their translator's hat each morning at the university gates" (35). Given the title of this book, it might seem intuitive that I would want to push back against this tendency by making myself more visible as a literary translator in this scholarly context. This is not, however, the approach that I take—for the most part. Not due to any institutional considerations, as widespread and as problematic as they are (I am fortunate to teach at one of the few colleges that currently recognize translation as intellectual work), but because my interest in the way that practices, practitioners, and theories of translation are being mobilized as a narrative element in contemporary fiction is more rhetorical than experiential. That said, I do break the fourth wall in the chapter on Mario Bellatin, which centers on a book that I translated, because I participated in Bellatin's theoretical game in a way that relates directly to the issues of authorship and appropriation here examined.

Talking about translation means being resigned to saying at once too little and too much. Too little, because the inherent capaciousness of the practice means that any attempt to fix it as an object of study will necessarily leave out much of what defines it. In this case, because the novels here examined tend to center on literary—rather than technical—translation, the increasingly theorized practice of localization as it pertains to the market dynamics of globalization will not be explored to the fullest; nor will translational practices such as code-switching and hybrid forms of discourse. Too much, because—despite the dislocations and circulations inherent to the practice—any instance of translation is fundamentally grounded in a specific cultural moment and the political, social, and aesthetic conditions that comprise it. To talk about translation as a general or even regional practice is always to some extent an effacement of that specificity. Acknowledging these limitations, this book aims to contribute new material from the Latin American literary landscape to the fictional turn in translation studies, and to elucidate the ways in which these works stage anti-neocolonial resistance to the conjoined notions of intellectual property and propriety and, in so doing, lay the foundations of a non-extractivist mode of reading works in translation.

1

Monsters and Parricides

Translation is the language of planets and monsters.
— Emily Apter, *The Translation Zone*

In the court of public opinion, translation faces a number of catchy indictments. Along with the appealingly consonant *traduttore, traditore*, the blithely anthropomorphic characterization *belles infidèles* suggests that translations—like women—can be either beautiful or faithful, but never both.[1] As Lori Chamberlain so compellingly observed, the libidinal anxiety evinced by this *bon mot* maps directly onto questions of legal legitimacy, both domestic and intellectual: whether expressed in Roscommon's genteel rhetoric of guardianship or George Steiner's sexualized terms of conquest, these gendered notions of translation reinforce, through a "cultural complicity between the issues of fidelity in translation and in marriage," the hierarchical system according to which a translation is publicly tried for crimes "an original (as husband, father, or author) … is by law incapable of committing" (1988: 456).[2]

---

[1] The phrase *belles infidèles* is attributed to Nicolas Perrot d'Ablancourt (1606-64), who used it in defense of his own paraphrastic translations of classical texts (qtd. Godayol 2013: 99). More recently, José Ortega y Gassett evoked this question of gender and fidelity in the title of his 1937 article "Miseria y esplendor de la traducción," a nod to Honoré de Balzac's *Splendeurs et misères des courtisanes*.

[2] Though gender plays a role in the discussion of the metaphor of reproduction, this is not an exploration of specifically *feminist* approaches to translation theory such as those proposed by critics and translators like Barbara Godard, Carol Maier, Sherry Simon, and Luise von Flotow. For an overview of this approach, see Melissa Wallace's 2002 article, "Writing the Wrongs of Literature."

Like so many moral imperatives, these injunctions against interlinguistic dalliance are not purely principled. With the inception of copyright in the early eighteenth century, the enforcement of intellectual propriety takes on a proprietary dimension, mimicking a "kinship system where paternity" or the masculinized act of creation "legitimizes an offspring" (1988: 456). In the domestic sphere, this legitimation is of principal importance to the transfer of title, to determining who is both responsible for and beneficiary of a property. The threat that lurks behind infidelity, then, on both the domestic and the literary level, is that of confusing or defusing these lines of descent and, subsequently, the categories of ownership that they uphold. When intellectual lineage—grounded either in a metaphorics that echoes sexual reproduction, whereby a masculine author-original begets a derivative, feminized, and potentially "treasonous" translation, or in the carbon-copy model presented by the rhetoric of cloning—is challenged by a translation that asserts its own creativity, the result is often rejected as illegitimate or monstrous.

Sometimes this monstrosity is shockingly ... cute. At least, it would be hard to describe the premise of Julio Cortázar's 1951 short story "Carta a una señorita en París" ["Letter to a Young Lady in Paris"] any other way. For Cortázar, who was himself a translator—he brought the work of Poe, Chesterton, Gide, and Yourcenar, among others, into Spanish, and translated for the United Nations Educational, Scientific, and Cultural Organization (UNESCO) during his years in Paris—translation and the negotiation of cultural and linguistic difference was a recurring theme.[3] The letter of the story's title is written by a

---

[3] For more on Cortázar's work as a translator and additional interpretations of "Letter to a Young Lady in Paris," see Stavans 1996 and Guzmán 2006. In her essay "Translation as Testimony: On Official Histories and Subversive Pedagogies in Cortázar," Adriana Pagano argues that this translational "not entirely belonging" affords the writer a dual perspective, and that Cortázar in turn presents translation in his fiction as "a *locus* of violence and tension: violence resulting from the imposition of words and meanings to translate reality; tension between the plurality of meanings that, though consciously suppressed, are always there, ready to challenge the most carefully planned transfer of meaning" (82).

translator who—in a spatialized metaphor of the dynamics of his profession—lives in one borrowed home after another. He is currently occupying a property in a well-heeled neighborhood of Buenos Aires that has been lent to him by a young woman named Andrea while she is away in Paris. As Rosemary Arrojo observes in her analysis of the story, this apartment serves as a metaphor for an original text into which the translator must insert himself: the space and all the objects contained therein are organized according to "un orden cerrado, construido ya hasta en las más finas mallas del aire" (2011: 17) [a compact order, built even to the finest nets of air (1998: 8)], where the narrator observes that everything "parece tan natural, como siempre que no se sabe la verdad" (18) [looks so natural, as always when one does not know the truth (8)]. The same way everything looks so natural when one accepts an author's narrative as a pure, unmediated account of their experience: a willing suspension of disbelief rarely afforded translations.

The first disruption of this carefully constructed order is the translator's replacement of a small metal tray with his English dictionaries, to keep them in easy reach; he feels great distress at needing to make this adjustment, and writes that moving the tray "altera el juego de relaciones de toda la casa, de cada objeto con otro, de cada momento de su alma con el alma entera de la casa y su habitante lejana" (2011: 18) [alters the play of relationships in the whole house, of each object with another, of each moment of their soul with the soul of the house and its absent inhabitant (1998: 8)]. No matter how hard he might try, the translator-tenant cannot help but leave his mark on the luxurious text-space he occupies, and the awareness of his own presence disturbs him.

Changing the place of a silver tray would hardly be anything to write home (or Paris) about, but the narrator of this story suffers from an unusual pathology that makes it impossible for him to occupy Andrea's property without leaving a trace: he periodically vomits up a small rabbit. Before he moved in, this would only happen once a month or so, leaving him plenty of time to give the animals away and keep their number under control. In the elevator on the day he arrives, however, the translator feels a little ball of fluff rising in his throat and he births the animal from his mouth.[4] The first rabbit is followed by another and another, until he finds himself in the uncomfortable position of needing to hide a dozen bunnies from his hostess's housekeeper and to repair the damage they're doing to her home—most notably, to her extensive library. After chewing through the spines of the books on the bottom shelf, they've moved up to the second. The flustered translator has no choice but to turn the books around, lest they be ruined.

In this elaborate metaphor of translation and its (illicit) relationship to authorship, these archetypically fertile little creatures stand in for the translator's creative impulse: an inconvenient presence that erupts within—and inevitably, inexorably, alters—the pristine and privileged sphere of the authored text. The translator first attempts to conceal the destruction, but his solution of repasting the book's bindings doesn't last long. "Anoche," he writes, "di vuelta a los libros del segundo estante; alcanzaban ya a ellos, parándose o saltando, royeron los lomos para afilarse los dientes" (2011: 27) [Last night, I turned the books on the second shelf in the other direction; they were already reaching that high, standing on their hind legs or jumping, they gnawed off the backs to sharpen their teeth (1998: 14)]. As the animals multiply and "sharpen their teeth" on the space of authorial attribution, the translator resorts to turning the books around, preserving the authorial mark but rendering it invisible, further confusing the provenance of the ideas contained within. The story ends on a tragic note when the narrator, realizing that he has lost control of the rabbits (his overactive creative impulse) and that he is taking up more and

---

[4] Cortázar uses the word "vomitar" to describe the process, but the image of the narrator sticking two fingers down his throat to help the rabbit out more closely resembles the use of forceps in childbirth.

more space, being more and more visible, decides to end his life by jumping from the balcony of Andrea's opulent apartment. This guilt, we are to understand, arises from his discovering himself so fecund and not, as is expected of his office, merely the vehicle of another's creativity.[5]

The connection between property, propriety, and textual filiation is already present in Friedrich Schleiermacher's foundational 1813 lecture, "On the Different Methods of Translating," in which the philosopher presents opposition between bringing the author to the reader (by making the forms of expression familiar to her) or bringing the reader to the author (by stretching the limits of the target language to accommodate structures from the source language).[6] According to Schleiermacher, this presents a real impasse for the translator. "Who would not like to make his native tongue appear everywhere displaying the most splendid characteristic beauty allowed by each genre?" he asks, before veering into a succession of metaphors that touch on the themes of lineage, property, and propriety (and the violence that runs through them all).

> Who would not prefer to beget children who would purely represent their fathers' lineage, rather than mongrels? ... Who would gladly consent to be considered ungainly for striving to adhere so closely to the foreign tongue as his own language allows, and to being criticized, like parents who entrust their children to tumblers for their education, for having failed to exercise his mother tongue in the sorts of gymnastics native to it, instead accustoming it to alien, unnatural contortions!
>
> (2012: 53)

---

[5] Rosemary Arrojo suggests that "the impossibility of reconciling his desire to express himself and his duty to preserve the author's composition is what constitutes the translator's tragedy," and goes on to point out that even when he is about to jump, "the translator is concerned about his posthumous visibility" (2018: 30).

[6] This dichotomy would later be formulated by Lawrence Venuti as *domesticating* and *foreignizing* translations. See also note 17 on page 74.

For Schleiermacher, translation is a family affair—and a fraught one, at that: it is striking how, in his attempt to find language for the translator's battle of aesthetic allegiances, his metaphors pile up and tangle the line of descent. First, the translator sires a form of language that risks accusations of being an ill-born "mongrel"—translated by Waltraud Bartscht in another edition of the text as "bastard," an interpretation that places greater emphasis on the themes of inheritance and lineage here explored, even as it misses the inflection of admixture so notable in the German "Blendlinge."[7] In the next image, the translator is again a parent figure, albeit a negligent one: rather than infidelity, the translator is now accused of giving the fruit of his labors-or-loins away to the circus, subjecting it to unnatural linguistic contortions (*Verrenkungen*). The series of metaphors ends with a marked generational slippage, whereby the transgressions of and against the child become an act of violence visited upon the mother tongue, specifically identified as such (*Muttersprache*).[8]

It is hardly a stretch to read these generational contortions through a Freudian lens, as Harold Bloom did in *The Anxiety of Influence*, claiming that authors view their predecessors according to the model of "father and son" facing off "as mighty opposites" (1973: 11).[9] These Oedipal dynamics prominent throughout are echoed in the gendered and reproductive metaphors examined in this chapter, and is also notable in the translation theory of the Brazilian translator, poet, and critic Haroldo de Campos, who describes the practice in terms of

---

[7] See Pym 1995 for more on this term.
[8] Pilar Godayol traces the diverse overlapping metaphors that connect gender dynamics with translation. "Over time," she writes, "there have been different models of sexual relationships in translation discourses such as that of the author (man) with the translation (woman), that of the translator (man) with the translation (woman), the friendship between the translator (man) and the author (man) characterized by the paternal attention paid by both to the translation (woman), the relationship between the author (man) and his mother tongue, or that between the translator (man) and the language of the original text (woman)" (2013: 100).
[9] Jorge Luis Borges, in "Los traductores de las *1001 noches*" ["The Translators of the *Thousand and One Nights*"], likewise presents the relation among different generations of translators of the storied text as one of "aniquilación" (397) [annihilation] and enmity among individuals and the aesthetic and ideological tendencies they represent.

filiation, transgression, and violence as "a parricidal dis-memory."[10] In his model, translation—specifically through its ties to the notion of intellectual inheritance—is the lever by which entrenched cultural hierarchies are overturned.

In their engagement of these filial dynamics through gendered or reproductive tropes of translation theory, the contemporary writers examined in this chapter not only create translator figures that establish themselves as "mighty opposites" to the authors they engage; some go a step further to posit these intercultural, intertextual relations as rhizomatic, rather than linear, phenomena that challenge the hierarchical dynamics outlined above. At their most extreme, these narratives center on figures of monstrosity and excess that—rather than serving as cautionary tales—undermine hierarchical notions of intellectual influence by erasing "the difference between production and reproduction which is essential to the establishment of power" (Chamberlain 1988: 466). These writers—who include Graciela Safranchik, Luis Fernando Verissimo, and César Aira—replace filial deference with parricidal defiance, creating the conditions necessary for a reconfiguration of the dyads of original and copy, creation and derivation, center and periphery.

I. Tea for One

The translator protagonist of Argentinean critic and playwright Graciela Safranchik's largely overlooked 1995 novella *El cangrejo* [The crab] shares with Cortázar's nomadic, rabbit-vomiting narrator a deep sense of isolation and a penchant for self-effacement. This short text centers on Akinari, a translator from the Japanese who specializes in invisible authors, those who have been "olvidados por la industria editorial" (Safranchik 1995: 45) [forgotten by the publishing industry]; he cherishes

---

[10] The term "desmemória parricida" appears in de Campos's *Deus e o Diabo no Fausto de Goethe* (São Paulo: Perspectiva, 1981). Quoted in Pires Vieira (1999: 97).

the "tarea solitaria" (45) [solitary task] of translation, and considers it compensation for the hours he spends teaching in order to pay his bills. Akinari dedicates the lion's share of his intellectual efforts—such as they are before he falls into the paralysis of an all-consuming infatuation with a woman he sees one day at his regular café—to the work of a seminal eighteenth-century Japanese scholar and writer named Ueda Akinari; this denominative doubling of the author by the translator is touched upon in various ways throughout. According to the narrator, Ueda was "totalmente eclipsado" (21) [completely eclipsed] by his work during his lifetime, and further dissipated his authorial presence by adopting multiple pseudonyms, which few scholars aside from his namesake translator ever traced back to him. As Akinari becomes more and more invested in Ueda's work, he begins to adopt these pseudonyms in his own scholarly writing, eclipsing himself in turn.

Like these bodies of work that flit into and out of visibility, the object of Akinari's desire, Miranda, is also an invisible being—even as her name evokes the notion of sight through its resonance with the Spanish verb "mirar," the act of looking or watching. In fact, the first time Akinari sees her, he doesn't: her face is deformed by an intense light shining on it from above. Rather than diminishing his impression of her, this distortion makes her even more appealing in Akinari's eyes. Miranda is later described as having "una forma muy extraña de moverse … Como una muñeca" (Safranchik 1995: 13) [a strange way of moving … Like a doll], and this observation arouses Akinari even more. Her gaze is "diáfana" (30) [diaphanous], her hair is "vaporosa," and her skin is "de una transparencia inusual" (32) [vaporous; unusually transparent]; her presence is so ephemeral that Akinari wonders, after fleeing the café in a state of emotional turmoil, if she ever existed in the first place, or if he invented her. This disturbing characterization culminates in the narrator's observation that Miranda's features seem like drawings, and he "tuvo la sensación de que él mismo podía modificarlos a su antojo" (32) [he sensed he could modify them as he wished].

Just as the invisibility and mutability of Akinari and Miranda resonate with tropes of solitude and sterility that posit the translator as a body which cannot create a lineage of his own, there is also a textual sterility tied up in the structure of his desire for her. Not only does Akinari's work come crashing to a halt as he progressively loses himself to his infatuation with Miranda, he fantasizes about writing her letters in the specific hope that she never responds to them (44). Like the ephemeral image he constructs of the object of his desire, his missives of love are by design instances of linguistic onanism, pure projection.

This linguistic sterility turns out to be genetic: though Akinari's father had been a language instructor, his mother—for whom Japanese was a second language—was prone to verbal externalizations that never became communication, simply repeating words "como quien acomodaba flores en un ramo" (Safranchik 1995: 67–8) [like someone arranging flowers in a bouquet]. From that union came Akinari, "el bromista, el gran farfullador" (69) [the joker, the great stammerer]. These monikers, of course, are not his: they belong to the other Akinari—Ueda—whose own family tree is even more gnarled. In keeping with scholarly accounts of Ueda's life, the novel states that the scholar and poet was taken in as a young child by wealthy merchants, according to a practice whereby any family unable to produce a male heir would simply adopt one (38). This fact illuminates and complicates one of the pseudonyms Ueda assigns himself, which in turn ties directly to the tropes examined in this chapter: Tarô the translator. As Akinari points out, Tarô is a name assigned to a family's firstborn, but "que habitualmente está asociado a Jirô y a Saburô, el Segundo y el tercer hijo" (38) [which usually appears alongside a Jirô and a Saburô, a second and third son]. As a result, "Ueda se presentaba como el mayor de un montón inexistente de hermanos de una familia que no les daba nombre, sino que se limitaba a contarlos" (38) [Ueda presented himself as the eldest among a bunch of nonexistent siblings in a family that doesn't give them names, simply counting them instead]. In this way, Ueda's assumed name—which is in turn assumed by Akinari—puts emphasis on the gaps in the family line, on the fact that, as a transplant, his roots barely enter the soil of the family tree to which he is now attached.

The association of chimeric kinship and fragmented lineage with the identity of the translator is reinforced by the juxtaposition of this moniker with another key pseudonym used by Ueda—one Akinari is too intimidated to adopt because in it he can feel the "presencia ominosa de su predecesor" (Safranchik 1995: 22) [ominous presence of his predecessor] weighing on him "como una amenaza" (22) [like a threat]. It is the pseudonym that provides the novel's title: *El cangrejo* [The crab]. Standing in clear opposition to the accumulating images of solitude and sterility, the Crab represents a virile, creative energy. It is the most authorial of the author's signs, the one aligned with writing. Even as Akinari reflects on how distant the figure feels from his own reality, he recognizes that it is the persona he would need to adopt in order to tell the story of his overpowering love, and indeed to become an agent within it. The Crab, he thinks, "despertando de pronto dentro suyo, sería quien contara la historia de la mujer. Lo dejaría hacer. Él sabría encontrar las palabras precisas" (24) [suddenly awakening within him, would be the one to tell the story of the woman. Akinari would let him. He would know how to find the right words].

In a sense, Akinari is right. In a twist at the end of the novel, which could plausibly be read as a continuation of the narrator's earlier fever dreams, Miranda appears at the translator's door. It is pouring outside (a nod, perhaps, to Ueda's *Harusame Monogatari*, or *Tales of Spring Rain*) and, again, between the rain in his eyes and the umbrella that covers hers, Akinari does not *see* Miranda until she is inside his apartment. She has read the letter he wrote her days earlier and— contrary to his fantasy—replied: first with a missive of her own that he received but never opened, and then with her physical presence, such as it is. As soon as she comes into view, however, "agitada y empapada por la lluvia, parada en su propio zaguán, riendo para él, tan hermosa," he discovers that "él no estaba allí, o se encontraba sorprendido en una fracción de tiempo diferente, dislocada del mundo" (1995: 94) [agitated and rain-soaked, standing on his doorstep, laughing for him, so beautiful ... he wasn't there, or he was caught in a different time, set apart from the world].

Just as Akinari and Miranda do and do not occupy the same physical space on the threshold of his home, they share a common language that seems at once tenuous and overdetermined. One of the first things Miranda says to Akinari, standing in his doorway, is that she is completely soaked. "Debí haber aprendido aquella frase que recitaba la serpiente" (1995: 96) [I must have learned that phrase the serpent would recite], she quips. Akinari laughs with her, even as he remarks to himself that she couldn't possibly have said what he thought he heard—a reference to the serpent in love that appears in a text by Ueda, which was inspired by the tenth-century *Ise Monogatari*.

> Sabía que desatinaba, que atribuía a esa mujer algo que solo estaba dentro de él ... Sin lugar a dudas, Miranda no podia imaginar hasta qué punto le hablaba a él en una lengua conocida, aun cuando intentase aludir a la tentación biblica.
>
> (96–7)
>
> He knew he was off base, that he was attributing to her something that was only inside him ... There was no way Miranda could imagine how much she was speaking to him in a familiar language, even if she were trying to allude to Biblical temptation.

Even at this climactic moment, the connection between the two is a projection on the part of Akinari, who connects Miranda's utterance—and, by extension, her—to a textual system near and dear to him.

This pattern is repeated moments later when Miranda enters, removes her sandals, and tosses them to the floor before saying to Akinari that, since her sandals were inside, she could stay. "Era más de lo que él podía atribuir al azar. ¿Conocía Miranda la historia de la heroína Kabuki que, escapando de su marido, arrojara las sandalias adentro del monasterio? ¿Quién era esta mujer que entraba así a su casa?" (1995: 97) [It was more than he could attribute to chance. Was Miranda familiar with the story of the Kabuki heroine who, fleeing from her husband, cast her sandals into the monastery? Who was this woman who entered his home this way?]. Who, indeed. If it's hard for Akinari to get a clear sense of Miranda, it's doubly difficult for the reader, thanks to the way he has been molding her all along to suit—and construct—his desire, both in terms of her physical aspect and as an intertextual surface onto which he projects the references that make up his own intellectual landscape.

This is beginning to sound familiar. In his eighteenth-century "Translation: A Poem," Thomas Francklin asserts, "Unless an author like a mistress warms, / How shall we hide his faults or taste his charms, / How all his modest latent beauties find ... Soften each blemish, and each grace improve, / And treat him with the dignity of Love?" (quoted in Chamberlain 1988: 457). Here, the translator dominates and shapes a feminized author-text with the express purpose of letting a more radiant version of him-her-it shine through. It is precisely this operation that Akinari performs on Miranda, whom he treats as a legible text. Even if that text is, like Ueda's work, occasionally hard to pin down or pull into focus.

The story ends with Akinari's second deferral of reading the letter Miranda wrote to him—that is, the second time he declines to engage the words and ideas generated by, rather than projected onto, her. The final words of the novel are "La tenía allí y no quería perderla" (1995: 99) [He had her there with him, and he didn't want to lose her]. Her "presence," then, is clearly linked to her effacement. Drawn specifically to the malleability he perceived in—or assigned to—her from the start, Akinari has finally succeeded in constructing Miranda out of textual material, the same way he pieced together his earlier writings on Ueda: looking for intertextual references, splicing them together, smoothing the seams. It seems, then, that it was not his writing a letter to Miranda that represents his assumption of the mantle of the Crab, but rather the writing of Miranda herself, which involves writing her into his story by re-writing (sometimes by completely ignoring) the words she puts into the world. Though it certainly chafes that the translator Akinari's discursive power is asserted through sustained symbolic violence enacted upon the character of Miranda, Safranchik's novel ultimately stakes this claim: Tarô the translator was the Crab, all along.

II. In the Name of the Father

The complex and often fraught dynamics of intellectual influence and homage also plays out in Brazilian writer Luis Fernando Verissimo's *Borges e os orangotangos eternos* (2000) [*Borges and the Eternal Orangutans* trans. Margaret Jull Costa 2004]; moreover, the threat of monstrous offspring that looms over Schleiermacher's remarks on translation is at the novel's heart—or, rather, its tail. Verissimo—who has worked as a translator, as well, though he is best known as a humorist—displays a dark sense of humor and a postmodern playfulness in this loosely epistolary, intensely intertextual, novel rich in allusions to the processes of coding and decoding inherent to translation. The novel follows a translator from Porto Alegre named Vogelstein, who—in his "vida enclausurada" (2000: 14) or "cloistered life" (2004: 4)—is another translator protagonist who seems to embody the stereotype of the scrivener unable to sire a work on his own. This stereotype is quickly overturned, however, when Vogelstein is assigned a story to translate for the Brazilian publication *Mistério Magazine*—a piece by "um tal Jorge Luis Borges, de quem eu ... nunca ouvira falar" (18) [a certain Jorge Luis Borges, of whom I ... had never heard (9)]. Finding the story "ruim, sem emoção e confuso" (18) [dreadful, confused, and lacking in excitement (9)], the enterprising young translator takes matters into his own hands, "improving" its weak ending by adding "alguns toques tétricos à moda de Poe à trama em um final completamente novo, surpreendente, que desmentia tudo o que viera antes, inclusive o relato do autor" (18) [a few lugubrious Poe-like touches to the plot and a completely new surprise ending that belied everything that had gone before, including the author's account of events (9)]. His modifications to the end of the work, of course, radically alter the original, retroactively setting it in opposition to the rules of the genre and turning its author, in his own angry words, into "o pior vilão que uma história policial pode ter: um narrador inconfiável" (19) [the worst villain a detective story can have: an unreliable narrator (10)]. In response to Vogelstein's insistence that he had merely performed the duties of a plastic surgeon undertaking a minor corrective procedure, the fictional version of Borges asserts that, instead of tinkering with the face of his text, Vogelstein had added "um rabo, uma 'cola' grotesca" (19) [a grotesque tail (10)] that is neither elegant nor functional. The letter attributes this transgression to the constitutional arrogance of translators, which, as it is hardly a typical indictment, may well be a nod on Verissimo's part to the Argentine writer's own translational activity.[11]

The grotesque tail to which the fictional Borges alludes at once epitomizes and reconstitutes the threat of monstrosity born of an unfaithful translation; Vogelstein's intervention directly contradicts the received notion that the translator is subserviently bound to the original. Significantly, this assertion of discursive authority is made precisely through the manipulation of the same gendered metaphorics of translation that traditionally privilege the original, insofar as the story's translational tail could easily be described as a displaced phallus. As Lori Chamberlain points out, "what the translator claims for 'himself' is precisely the right of paternity; he claims a phallus because this is the only way, in a patriarchal code, to claim legitimacy for the text" (1988: 466). Vogelstein's translation claims and also *resituates* this symbol of discursive authority.

The discursive violence against a literary father consolidated in this monstrous tail finds its literal complement as the novel progresses. Having learned, to his dismay, whose work he so cavalierly modified, Vogelstein stages an elaborate homage to the offended Argentine writer in the form of a grisly murder-inside-a-locked-room mystery as an apology for his translational gaffe. The scene of the crime is the Israfel Society Conference, a meeting of Edgar Allan Poe specialists, which is being held for the first time in Buenos Aires; the victim is the German scholar Joachim Rotkopf, a man with a

---

[11] As many critics, including Sergio Waisman (2005) and Efraín Kristal (2002), have observed, Borges had a similar penchant for modifying the texts he translated.

talent for making enemies who has publicly threatened to unmask one of the presenters at the conference as a fraud. When Rotkopf is found in a pool of blood in front of his full-length hotel room mirror, there is no shortage of suspects. In fact, for each symbol his body is thought to form with its reflection in the mirror (Vogelstein first remembers this shape as an X, then an O, followed by a W, an M and a parallelogram), a new murderer is declared. Throughout all this, Vogelstein stands happily by the side of the fictional Borges, offering suggestions and clues.

Both the murder and its investigation include myriad references to the work of Borges—most notably "Abenjacán el Bojarí, muerto en su laberinto" (1949) ["Ibn Hakkan Al-Bokhari, Dead in his Labyrinth"], from which Verissimo's novel draws its epigraph, and "La muerte y la brújula" (1942) ["Death and the Compass"].[12] Vogelstein has succeeded in translating intersemiotically the work of his idol into a grotesque *naturaleza muerta* [in English, a still life, but literally "dead nature"] composed of a few carefully placed playing cards, three knives hidden at different sites in the hotel (evoking the three points laid out by Scharlach to lead Erik Lönnrot to his fate in "La muerte y la brújula"), and the gory shifting signifier of the murder victim (which, again, maps onto the Tetragrammaton evoked in Borges's tale).[13] Here, too, we see an Oedipal challenge to the literary Father: whereas Borges laments the fact that he has only ever wielded *el fierro*, the blade as material associated with the representation of violence on the page, his self-appointed protégé takes up its counterpart, the active *vaivén*

---

[12] The intertextual references to Borges also extend to his readings of Poe, whose stories are mentioned as keys to the interpretation of the crime in Verissimo's novel; the detective in charge of the investigation is named Cuervo, Spanish for "raven" (again, the use of Spanish is significant here: in Portuguese it would be "corvo.") There is also the matter of the German's name, Rotkopf, which extends—through the evocation of the color red—the parallelism between the nemeses Lönnrot and Red Scharlach in Borges's "La muerte y la brújula," which in turn contains a reference to Poe's "Murders in the Rue Morgue."
[13] The concept of intersemiotic translation, or the movement between sign systems, was developed by Roman Jackobson in his 1959 essay "On Linguistic Aspects of Translation."

(85; the term, is presented in Spanish in Verissimo's Portuguese text, pointing to Borges's own usage).[14] The Oedipal aspect of the struggle over the denouement of the translated story that sparks Rotkopf's murder surfaces again in the revelation that the man sacrificed at the altar of literary-filial piety is in fact Vogelstein's biological father, who allowed his mother to be taken to the concentration camps in Germany during World War II. Significantly, the truth about Vogelstein's parentage is revealed in an epistolary tail appended to the narrative (presented under the Spanish-language heading "La cola"), as the final word in the novel ceded to the fictional Borges by his repentant translator. This second tail very much mirrors the first, particularly in the way it undermines the reliability of the text's narrator and, in the process, reconstitutes the author sign to which the work is attached. The closing lines of the novel, in fact, are spent chiding Vogelstein (or, more accurately, Verissimo himself) for his lack of attention to detail, as the fictional Borges breaks the fourth wall to explain that the only story he ever published in *Mistério Magazine* came out in 1948, meaning that, "a não ser que fosse um prodígio de precocidade" (130) [unless you were a marvel of precocity (131)], Vogelstein could not possibly have translated it.

Despite all its intertextual irreverence, there is a limit to how far this novel subverts linear models of intellectual influence and the sanctity of the original. Whereas its first tail destabilized the oeuvre of a canonical literary father (albeit by appealing to the same structures of discursive power that endowed the original with its authority), these final corrective remarks constitute not only a performance of the discursive authority of the canonical figure invoked, they also insist on the author's control in a broad sense: after marveling for a moment at the unusual gesture of allowing a character to determine the ending of

---

[14] "Vaivén" is a lovely noun composed of the elements "va y viene" [go and come], which translates as a "back and forth" and can be used to describe many things, including the slashing or jabbing motion of a blade. In the afterword to *Borges, Between History and Eternity*, Hernán Diaz discusses Borges's elaboration on the term "vaivén" in a 1967 interview with *The Paris Review*. For more on this image of the "flash of the knife, the sudden flash," see Díaz (2012: 161).

a work, the fictional Borges observes that "nunca escapamos do autor, por mais generoso ou penitente que ele pareça" (119) [we never escape the author, no matter how generous or penitent he may seem (121)]. The boundless influence of the author suggested here reinforces a general adherence to vertical, gendered models of discursive authority epitomized by the Oedipal dynamics found throughout.

That said, and even taking into consideration the novel's mobilization of phallogocentric models of discursive authority, *Borges e os orangotangos eternos* cannot be entirely subsumed within patrilinear structures of intellectual influence. The novel's title supports this less conservative reading, insofar as it evokes both the solution to Poe's seminal locked-room mystery, "The Murders in the Rue Morgue" (1841), and—in the agelessness of its eponymous primates—the Infinite Monkey Theorem, the most common formulation of which asserts that it is, in fact, not statistically impossible for a monkey sitting at a keyboard and hitting keys at random to eventually produce *Hamlet*. Though principally a reflection on the cumulative probability of a string of independent events, the Theorem unsettles the notion of authorial genius by framing this seminal work as the statistically possible, if not entirely probable, outcome of a repetitive mechanical action.

This destabilizing gesture plays out, as illustrated above, in the relationship between original and translation in the opening pages of the novel; it also inflects the Oedipal violence of Rotkopf's murder. Whereas Vogelstein's assertion of power in adding a narrative "tail" to Borges's story resituates discursive authority without undermining the hierarchical structures from which it is derived, his second translation—which renders Borges's forays into detective fiction as a very real mystery—turns the body of the father into a sign that does not impose meaning from above, but instead actively resists comprehension. Because the staging of Rotkopf's corpse is conceived from the outset to provide a series of false clues, the body of the father thus comes to *em*body hermeneutic indeterminacy, the intersection of divergent outcomes and thus the impossibility of establishing a single, authoritative version of the story.

III. Of Bastards and Clones

If the model of productive monstrosity presented by Luis Fernando Verissimo destabilizes but does not entirely dismantle the phallogocentrism inherent to gendered metaphorics of translation, the science of biogenetics provides another arena in which to contend with these entrenched discursive hierarchies. In *The Translation Zone* (2006), Emily Apter presents a metaphor of textual re/production meant to subvert models of intellectual filiation that posit translation as a secondary practice tied to the notion of (cultural) dependency. Rather than reading translation through the lens of gender politics, Apter homes in on the metaphor of biological coding and transfer behind the technology of cloning by way of the concept of pseudotranslation, or what she refers to as "translation with no original" (2006: 212), which constitutes itself of genetic material from a donor tradition and in so doing passes itself off as kin. According to Apter, pseudotranslation can be seen as "the premier illustration of deconstructed ontology, insofar as it reveals the extent to which all translations are unreliable transmitters of the original" and a point of articulation between "connoisseur wars" and the question of whether all translations, by their very nature, are "born not from a 'real' original, understood as an authenticated work by a recognized author, but from a kind of 'test tube' of simulated originality" (2006: 212-13).[15]

Despite this disruptive potential, the baseline premise of pseudotranslation invites textual analysis expressed in terms of fraud and veracity, while the metaphor of translation as cloning—as presented above—ultimately posits a narrow conception of fidelity and presents textual monstrosity as its improper other. Though the examples of pseudotranslation cited by Apter exhibit absolute (albeit ethically problematic) freedom in terms of what they propose translation is and can be, little is said of the tension between this freedom and

---

[15] Note the echoes of cultural markets in the phrase "connoisseur wars."

the importance of rendering biogenetic code exactly according to its blueprint, which defines the science of cloning.[16]

In the *New York Times* article cited by Apter, which incidentally focuses on the *failures* of cloning in the early years of the Millennium, science journalist Gina Kolata describes cloning as the practice of making genetic material take root in a host body divested of its genetic identity. This description, of course, raises several questions. First, the idea of a cell emptied of its constitutive genetic makeup is no small matter in the discussion of translated literature and cultural politics—indeed, it pushes the notion of cultural exchange back in the direction of the privileged original and the subordinate copy. There is also the question of what allowance, if any, is made for the positive, *transcreational* intervention of the translator. As mainstream media dutifully remind us, terrible things happen when creativity is introduced into the transmission of biogenetic code, namely the generation of monstrous forms that are all the more horrifying for the way they simultaneously suggest and profane the bodies they are meant to reproduce.

Though the use of cloning as a metaphor for translation risks proliferating assessments of the practice grounded in achieving a technically impossible identity with a privileged original, César Aira manages to turn this model on end. In his 1999 novel *El congreso de literatura* [*The Literary Conference* trans. Katherine Silver 2010], Aira reframes the looming association of creative deviation with monstrosity—in genetic cloning as in translation—to transform the

---

[16] Though her study does not engage the specific metaphors of cloning explored here, Ulrike Orloff presents an interesting argument about the relevance of new reproductive technologies (NRTs) to the discussion of translation, insofar as this "mechanical" reproduction allows us to move away from gendered frameworks, and to begin to think of translation in terms of the rightful custody of the "best provider of care" for the text. According to Orloff, "Because of NRTs we have entered into an actual age of 'mechanical' human reproduction ... Instead of being based on the ideal of *automatic* rights, duties and responsibilities caused by heterosexual necessity and a romantic/sentimental ideology of biological kinship, parenthood can be based on the notion of *care*" (2005: 152).

hierarchical model of intellectual influence into a non-hierarchical network of proliferation and iteration.

Aira, like many of the writers who engage translation thematically in their work, has both translated extensively and reflected on the practice in essays and interviews. In a 2009 conversation with the Mexican essayist and translator Pablo Duarte for *Letras Libres*, Aira claims somewhat evasively that when he was most active as a translator, he approached the practice with "complete pragmatism," specializing in bestsellers because hackneyed prose is much quicker to render. Nonetheless, he also describes translating two plays by William Shakespeare, *Cymbeline* and *Love's Labour's Lost*, with almost masochistic glee, focusing—as he does in his reflections on the poetry of Edward Lear—on the qualities that make them untranslatable.

Nor is *El congreso de literatura* Aira's only novel that addresses the subject of translation: *El juego de los mundos* (2000) [The game of worlds] takes place in a world in which literature has been replaced by its translation into strings of phonetically associative ideograms that then need to be re-translated into narrative form, while *La Princesa Primavera* (2003) [Princess Springtime], which will be examined in Chapter 4, centers on a translator who lives in isolation on a remote island. Nonetheless, translation is of structural importance in *El congreso de literatura* to an extent that seems extraordinary, even for a writer as invested in metafictional gambits and wordplay as Aira. At the outset, the narrator identifies himself as a translator and draws a connection between his fiscal difficulties and the lagging interest in literature—particularly in translated works—and the financial crisis that shook the Argentine economy at the turn of the twenty-first century, demonstrating a conscious connection between the thematic material of the novel and the material conditions of a specific historico-economic context.[17]

---

[17] This is a reference to the failed neoliberal policies of Carlos Menem, President of Argentina from 1989 to 1999, and his successors, which led to an economic crisis marked by massive inflation and the *corralito*, a series of restrictions that froze access to bank accounts as the country's currency devalued.

Translation is presented as central not only to the plot, but also to the way the narrative unfolds. The novel opens with a prologue that outlines "el comienzo que hizo posible que hubiera una historia" (1999: 27) [the beginning that made it possible for there to be a story at all (2010: 17)]—that is, an account of how its translator protagonist comes into the fortune that solves his solvency problem and allows him to realize the plan on which the novel centers. As is the case with much of Aira's work, the plot can be summarized in a few lines, though its details would take volumes to fully explore. The narrator, who is at once a writer, translator, and mad scientist, has long wanted to clone a genius—it is crucial that his subject be a genius because our translator-mad scientist wants to follow, rather than lead, the legions of his creation. He sets his sights on Carlos Fuentes, who will be speaking at a literary conference in Venezuela, and creates a special biological device based on the DNA of a wasp to extract genetic material from the writer. The plan goes terribly awry, however, when the wasp takes a sample from Fuentes's necktie and the narrator unwittingly unleashes legions of enormous blue silkworms that descend on the site of the conference, leaving a trail of destruction in their wake.[18]

In the broadest sense, then, *El congreso de literatura* explores the pitfalls of servile relations to literary models. The central premise of the narrator's desire to create an army of clones he can follow rather than lead is funny precisely for the way it puts scientific industriousness at the service of intellectual passivity. Aira does, however, offer an

---

[18] This sequence includes a jab at both academic criticism and the structures of discursive authority, in the form of a nod to Foucault's concept of the author-function, which exists outside the text but determines the range of its possible interpretations, as well as the future discourse that can come of it. As Aira wryly asserts, "En realidad, no podía culparla ... ¿Cómo iba a saber ese pobre instrumento clónico descartable dónde terminaba el hombre y empezaba su ropa? Para ella era todo lo mismo, era todo 'Carlos Fuentes.' Al fin de cuentas, no era distinto lo que pasaba con los críticos y profesores que asistían al congreso, que se habrían visto en dificultades para decir dónde terminaba el hombre y dónde empezaban sus libros" (111). [I couldn't blame her ... how could that poor disposable cloned tool know where the man stopped and his clothing began? For her, it was all one, it was all "Carlos Fuentes." After all, it was no different than what happened when the critics and professors who were attending the conference found it difficult to say where the man ended and his books began (79).]

alternative to this verticality, and he does so precisely through the figure of monstrous cloning, the unfaithful translation. Early on, he refers to the narrative as a series of "translations" (presented in scare quotes throughout). In thinking about how to structure his tale, the narrator decides to

> empezar por la Fábula que constituye la lógica del relato. Después tendré que hacer la "traducción", pero como hacerlo completamente me llevaría más páginas de las que me he impuesto como máximo para este libro, iré "traduciendo" sólo donde sea necesario; donde no sea así, quedarán fragmentos de Fábula en su lengua original ... la Fábula a su vez toma su lógica de una Fábula anterior, en otro nivel más de discurso, del mismo modo que del otro lado la historia sirve de lógica inmanente de otra historia, y así al infinito.
>
> (1999: 27)
>
> begin with the Fable that provides the tale's logic. I will then have to do a "translation," which, if carried out in full, would take more pages than I have assigned as the maximum for this book; thus I will "translate" only when necessary; all other fragments of the Fable will remain in the original language ... the Fable in question takes its logic from a prior Fable, on yet another level of discourse; similarly on the other end, the story provides the immanent logic to another story, thus ad infinitum.
>
> (2010: 18)

This conceit, justified as a means of keeping the work to a manageable length, presents the novel as a discursive hodgepodge of "original" and "translated" text spliced together like so much DNA. To borrow an image from the canon of bio-manipulation, it is a tale fashioned after Frankenstein's monster.

The first of these "translations" reveals that the writer-translator who narrates the work is also the mad scientist described in its first chapter. This revelation establishes a connection between the narrator's literary activities and his work with biogenetics. Carlos Fuentes, it turns out, is not our translator protagonist's first experience with cloning. To the contrary, the matter has occupied his mind for some time: even before his first (not entirely successful) attempts to reproduce living subjects, he wrote a play about the matter. This play, which is staged during the conference, centers on the story of Adam and Eve, whose formation from Adam's rib is described by the narrator as history's first case of cloning. This story, he claims, "da pie por sí sola a la genética" (1999: 71) [gives rise to genetics (2010: 51)] by reducing all of humanity to a single point of origin, and is therefore also "the genesis of diversity," but—as the narrator points out, "if diversity has nobody on whom to spread itself out, it turns on itself, gets tangled up in its own general particularity, and therein the imagination is born" (51). This tangle of general particularity that gives rise to the imagination will take center stage as our translator-mad scientist's experiments with cloning spiral further and further out of control.

But back to Adam and Eve. In Aira's play, this seminal history is further complicated by the introduction of a new element: Adam has a wife at home who, though never seen on stage, interferes with his love for Eve. Unsurprisingly, this conceit proves to be (onto)logically thorny. As the playwright-translator-mad scientist himself admits, "si Adán y Eva eran respectivamente el único hombre y la única mujer en el planeta, entonces la esposa de Adán, la esposa ausente cuya existencia le impedía vivir su amor con Eva, no era otra que la misma Eva" (1999: 80) [if Adam and Eve were, respectively, the only man and the only woman on the planet, then Adam's wife—the absent wife who prevented him from living out his love with Eve—couldn't be anyone other than Eve herself (2010: 58)].

In other words, through his play the translator-mad scientist reimagines the lines of human filiation and, in so doing, jumbles them at their point of origin. Not only is cloning presented as the original form of reproduction—the genetic sample taken from the rib to create another being in the image of the first—the sexual reproduction of this original pair, the secondary form by which all of humanity is thought to have come into being, is radically destabilized. By multiplying this most entrenched point of origin (in the Judeo-Christian tradition, that is) and thereby rendering it unstable and diffuse, the novel proposes a second history of humanity parallel to the first that, while not usurping its place, precludes the linear logic of descent that governs it. In fact, this gesture is all the more destabilizing because the new version does not overwrite the old, but rather exists alongside it in an evocative state of conjunction. Again, though perhaps in a way not even Lori Chamberlain might have imagined, infidelity generates hermeneutic instability.

Infidelity and deviation, so maligned in biogenetics and conservative notions of translation, thus loom large over Aira's novel; here, however, deviation is ultimately the key to establishing a positive valence for cloning as a metaphor of translation. It is revealed early on that the products of the mad scientist's experiments are, paradoxically, "clones no parecidos" (1999: 28) [non-similar clones (2010: 18)]. The paragraph cited above, which injects the logic of the fable into the novel, describes a scientist not yet identified as "mad" engaged in the practice of cloning:

> el éxito era invariable, aunque al pasar a los seres humanos los clones resultantes cambiaron sutilmente de naturaleza: eran clones no parecidos. Superó el desaliento producido por esta variación diciéndose que al fin de cuentas la percepción de parecidos es algo muy subjetivo, siempre cuestionable. De lo que no tenía dudas era de que sus clones eran genuinos, legiones de Uno cuyo número podía multiplicar cuantas veces quisiera.
>
> (1999: 28)

> His success did not vary, though as he approached human beings the nature of the clones subtly changed; they became non-similar clones. He overcame his disappointment with this variation by telling himself that in the final analysis the perception of similarity is quite subjective and always questionable. He had no doubt, however, that his clones were genuine, legions of Ones whose numbers he could multiply as often as he wished.
>
> (2010: 18)

In addition to foregrounding the criteria by which identity among iterations is evaluated, and effectively dismantling the notion of fidelity by presenting similarity as subjectively, historically, and culturally contingent, Aira opens up a unique space in which translation can conduct its creative experiments. This is accomplished through the introduction of the non-identical clone that is, nonetheless, a "success"—a gesture that is repeated in the narrator's description of the miniscule "wasp" designed to extract DNA from Carlos Fuentes. The identification of this miniature insect, it turns out, with its genetic donor is "una simplificación abusiva" (54) [an abusive oversimplification (37)], given the clone's miniscule scale and composite physical form. What is the status of these duplicates-with-a-difference? What is this element that escapes the coding process yet is neither gained nor lost in transmission? Aira does not expand on the nature of this deviation, but the premise is no less telling for his silence; this quality of difference-within-similarity reveals the connection between the clones and the translations for which they serve as a metaphor, and hints at the subversive implications of this model of (re)production.

As a complement to his reflections on non-similar clones, the narrator offers a glimpse into the workings of his "hyperkinetic" mind, and—in so doing—greater insight into the relation between translation and cloning in the novel.[19] Everything, he says, "es metáfora en la microscopía hiperkinética de mi psiquis, todo está en lugar de otra cosa ... Bajo mi lupa interior," he writes, "o dentro de ella, cada pensamiento en su anamorfosis retórica toma la figura de un clon, una identidad sobredeterminada" (43) [is a metaphor in the hyperkinetic microscope of my psyche, everything is instead of something else ... Under my interior magnifying glass, or inside it, each thought takes on the guise of a clone in its rhetorical anamorphosis: an overdetermined identity (29)]. In addition to the figures of miniaturization and cloning, Aira renders the etymological origins of the figure of metaphor—the

---

[19] This "hyperkinesis" is explicitly associated in the novel with Aira's trademark "huida hacia adelante" [flight forward], the attested practice of never revising his work, of improvising his way from scenario to scenario until he reaches the end of a story. As a model of rampant textual proliferation, it also ties back in with the proliferation of non-similar clones.

Greek *metapherein*, or bearing across of a term or image into another space (which articulates neatly with the Latin *translatio* and, ultimately, the modern terms translation, *traducción* and the other variants derived from the Latin *traducere*, *übersetzen*, and so on)[20]—in a literal way, emphasizing the displacement of individual terms from one conceptual space to another. Translation, thus understood in terms of metaphor and displacement, endows each concept with the "overdetermined identity" of a clone.

The implications of the way translation and cloning operate independently and as metaphors for one another within the literary system of *El congreso de literatura* thus begin to come into focus. In the novel, deviation is a constitutive part of the cloning process, and does not imply a failure of any kind—we recall that the mad scientist considers his "clones no parecidos" to be part of his "invariable" success. The legion of "monstruos" (104, 123) [monsters] that descends upon the city of Mérida, where the conference takes place, is not the result of an experiment gone awry, but is rather the ideal outcome of the cloning process (or Aira's version of it, at least). "Lo veía con una claridad meridiana," he writes, "la célula de la seda contenía el ADN del gusano que la había producido, y el clonador, *funcionando a la perfección*, no había hecho más que descodificar y recodificar la información" (111-12, my italics) [I saw it with the clarity of the noonday sun: the silk cell contained the DNA of the worm that had produced it, and the cloning machine, functioning perfectly, had done nothing more than decode and recode the information (81)]. Monstrosity, in other words, does not exist in opposition to the "success" of the venture, but is rather its essence. It also typifies that tangle of generalized particularity—which we first saw in the narrator's theatrical adaptation of Genesis—wherein imagination is born.

---

[20] Curiously, one of the original uses of the term "translatio" was to discuss botanical grafting—a practice not unlike cloning insofar as it entails the proliferation of a single biological entity, as opposed to the sexual-reproductive model, which involves the selection and combination of genetic material. For more, see Umberto Eco's *Experiences in Translation* (2000: 74-5).

It is no coincidence, then, that silkworms are the end product of this process. Rather than an army of Fuentes clones that pay homage to a literary "genius" (at the same time their plurality undermines the Romantic category of genius itself), the cloning device—"functioning perfectly"—lets loose a horde of creatures that are creators in their own right. The genetic translation of Carlos Fuentes, which could have represented the height of intellectual passivity, thus becomes a parallel figure of production, reminding us once again of Haroldo de Campos's concept of *transcriação* and its defense of translations as independent, fecund cultural objects. Aira's description of these silkworms itself is also significant, insofar as it corresponds to the motif of scale in the novel, and casts the translational metaphor developed therein in a new light. Though the cloned silkworms are exponentially larger than their "originals," Aira often gravitates toward the miniature, as is the case with the tiny "wasp."

In *Espectáculos de realidad* [Spectacles of reality], Reinaldo Laddaga homes in on what Aira himself identifies in the work of the writer and cartoonist Copi as a "pasión por miniaturizar" (2007: 116) [passion for miniaturization] and explores its relevance to Aira's own writing. Even before the publication of *El congreso de literatura*, his fascination with multiplication and miniatures can be seen in the short story "Las dos muñecas" ["The Two Dolls"], part of the 1998 collection *La trompeta de mimbre* [The wicker *trumpet*]. In the story, Eva Perón has two perfect miniatures of herself fashioned in order to be able to make more public appearances. Like the silkworms in *El congreso de literatura*, the "dolls" are perfect non-identical replicas: they are "asombrosamente pequeñas, pero las medidas estaban bien tomadas, y respondían hasta el último milímetro al modelo" (152) [astonishingly small, though their measurements were taken well and corresponded to the model, down to the last millimeter]. Though the exuberant audience at the events gives no sign of recognizing the trick—the crowds, thrilled by the presence of Evita, "la agigantaban" (152) [enlarged her], compensating for the difference in scale—the force and meaning of Evita's physical presence, her status as unifying origin of a political movement and a cultural imaginary, is ultimately revealed as a mirage when one of the dolls malfunctions and the sleight of hand is revealed.

According to Laddaga, this miniaturization is characterized by the invocation of small details in the service of presenting "un mundo remoto o próximo como exótico, pero también mostrarlo como *absolutamente denso*, recargado" (2007: 116, my italics) [a distant or nearby world as exotic, but also revealing it as absolutely dense, overloaded].[21] Enormous as they are, the silkworms that the translator-mad scientist of *El congreso de literatura* unleashes on Mérida are no different: observing one of them, the narrator remarks that, despite its size, it "[seguía] siendo una miniature" (1999: 123) [was still a miniature (2010: 90)]; the silkworms, like all clones, recreate "en pequeño toda la geología de la evolución de la vida" (37) [on a small scale the entire geology of the evolution of life (25)]. It is in this quality of being miniature, understood in the work of Aira as an "absolute density," that the clone represents "una identidad sobredeterminada" (2010: 29) [an overdetermined identity].

This reading, in turn, underscores the overlap between the set of traits and behaviors that make up an identity, and the condition of being identical, precisely that part of the identity of the clone that is called into question in this novel. In *El congreso de literatura*, this absolute density is inseparable from the notion of proliferation. The silkworms of the novel's denouement represent a non-hierarchical multiplicity in two different ways: first, by short-circuiting the idea that a "translation" need be subordinate to its "original" (the clone is an immense version of the source of the silk from which its DNA was retrieved), and second, by creating a legion of these producers within which any two members are interchangeable. In this way, Aira brings the metaphor of translation as cloning into uncharted territory,

---

[21] Aira shares this enthusiasm for the miniature with Walter Benjamin; as Hannah Arendt points out in her introduction to *Illuminations*, Benjamin "had a passion for small, even minute things ... For him the size of an object was in an inverse ratio to its significance ... The smaller the object, the more likely it seemed that it could contain in the most concentrated form everything else" (1969: 11–12).

systematically emptying out the notion of an authoritative point of origin from which multiple versions descend.

There is much here that evokes the figure of the rhizome developed by Gilles Deleuze and Félix Guattari in *A Thousand Plateaus: Capitalism and Schizophrenia*, particularly in the concept of the multiplicity.[22] Like the silkworms that descend upon Mérida from all directions, the multiplicity, a substantive entity in and of itself, has "neither a subject nor an object, only determinations, magnitudes, and dimensions" (1987: 8). The figure of the strong principal unity, which the rhizome exposes and supplants, is readily mapped onto conservative models of translation: the "Tree or Root as an image" that "endlessly develops the law of the One that becomes two, then of the two that become four" (5) perpetuates those models of translation that privilege the original text over its subsequent iterations, which are in turn viewed as derivative.

Even when they are praised for being creative, adventurous, or innovative, translated works within an arboreal system are subject to evaluation in relation to a privileged original. Not so in the rhizomatic model of translation presented by Aira through his particular approach to the metaphor of cloning, which knocks this entire evaluative system off its axis. More accurately, it does away with the idea of an axis entirely; the point or origin is impossible to locate because any and every iteration can be the origin of any other. Indeed, the rhizome presents an alternative to "arborescent pseudomultiplicities" (8) that are in fact "hierarchical systems with centers of significance and subjectification" (16). Instead, the principles of heterogeneity and interconnectivity shape its system of relations as alliances, conjunctions: "The tree is filiation, but the rhizome is alliance, uniquely alliance. The tree imposes the verb 'to be,' but the fabric of the rhizome is conjunction, 'and … and … and'" (25). Rather than paying homage to an authoritative intellectual

---

[22] Aira raises the connection to Deleuze and Guattari—sardonically, it should be said—in the interview with Pablo Duarte mentioned above; for more on the critique of capitalism embedded in much of Aira's work, see Reber 2007.

progenitor, and in so doing, becoming rooted in a fixed (subordinate) position on the spectrum of discursive authority and proprietorship, the rhizomatic text forms multiple, dynamic alliances. It is in this sense, too, that Aira's "clones no parecidos" can be considered successes: the measure of their value has been uncoupled from questions of fidelity to a privileged original.

Given Aira's insistence on the reciprocal, associative, and horizontal nature of translation, developed through the literary mobilization of cloning as a metaphor for the practice, his assertion that the full potential of an idea is only realized through its "pasaje a otro cerebro" (32) [passing through another brain (21)] offers a fitting conclusion to these reflections. Both *Borges e os orangotangos eternos* and *El congreso de literatura* are ultimately grounded in this notion; both insist that is not faithful *repetition* (in translation, that problematic holy grail of the transparent pane through which to glimpse the original) that brings out the value of an idea or work, but rather the *variation* inherent to its gestation in the mind of the other. Both valorize the reproduction of texts, beings, and ideas alike under the productive sign of (monstrous) deviation.

This is not to say that any of these three writers entirely eschew the trappings of literary consecration; to the contrary, one of the narrative gestures that unite these novels is the invocation of canonical literary figures as characters. It bears noting, of course, that these intellectual idols do not hail from across the Atlantic but are in two cases part of the Latin American literary tradition, and in the third, a major figure in Japanese literature. In the context of a system of deference and allusion that has historically privileged European cultural authority, this shift is not without significance (nor is the irreverence with which two out of three are treated). Furthermore, enacting the metaphorics of productive monstrosities that challenge intellectual influence and derivation, both Aira's and Verissimo's novels destabilize the author-signs they invoke by inventing works and biographical data and inserting them into the oeuvre associated with each one.

Another thematic thread that unites two of these three novels is the fact that the action of each unfolds, to a large extent, within the institutional space of the literary conference, which further resonates with the themes of cultural legitimation and the hierarchical dynamics of global cultural exchange explored in the preceding pages. Through their mobilizations of gendered and reproductive metaphors for translation, all three of these novels empty out the concept of translation as derivative, interrogating the status and function of the original, valorizing translation as an independent creative act, and ultimately offering new, reciprocal models of production beyond the influence of influence.

2

Foreign Correspondence

Homonymie n'est pas synonymie.
　　　　　　　　　—Maxime Koessler, *Les Faux Amis*

Friendship engages translation in the untranslatable.
　　　　　　　—Jacques Derrida, *The Politics of Friendship*

In the fall of 2016, the moviegoing public was given a crash course in the philosophy of language in the form of a blockbuster called *Arrival*, based on a novella by Ted Chiang.[1] Its premise is as follows: when twelve spacecraft install themselves at different locations around the world, a linguistics professor is called in to save the day—that is, to establish communication with the visitors in the hope of avoiding an interplanetary apocalypse. Communication, of course, is never a straightforward process, much less under these circumstances: even after establishing a basic shared vocabulary, divergent translations of a key term nearly lead to catastrophe when interpretations differ as to whether an object mentioned by the visitors is being presented as a tool or a weapon. Above and beyond this *mise en scène* of the mechanisms and limits of translation, *Arrival* is an ode to the theory of linguistic relativity. As soon as the linguist acquires (in the proprietary rhetoric commonly applied to proficiency) this extraterrestrial language, which is based on simultaneity rather than sequential progression, she discovers that her relationship to the world around her—and to the linear conception

---

[1] The film, directed by Denis Villeneuve, is based on *Story of Your Life* by Ted Chiang, who spent five years studying linguistics before sitting down to write. See Ulaby 2016.

of time according to which it is organized—has changed. With her consciousness no longer tethered to the mutual exclusivity of past, present, and future that sustains the grammar of her mother tongue, her consciousness is able to move between these temporalities with relative ease and she finds herself living in multiple timelines at once. Whereas geopolitical context determined the interpretation of a single sign in the different languages of Earth, the extraterrestrial language brought with it an entirely new way of being in the world.

If we were to have stood very close to one of the state-of-the-art speakers in that darkened theater, training our ear on the static emanating from somewhere inside it, we might have made out the soft crinkle of wool and the echoes of a few familiar voices discussing the ways language systems are both shaped by, and determinate of, the contexts in which they arise, and what effects these differences have on patterns and horizons of thought. We might have caught a few phrases from Leibniz, or overheard Wilhelm von Humboldt discussing the incommensurability of languages and the worldviews that attend them. Perhaps we would have discerned snippets of Borges's "La busca de Averroes" (1947) ["Averroes's Search"] or heard Wittgenstein intone: "The limits of my language mean the limits of my world." Edward Sapir or Benjamin Lee Whorf might even have chimed in.[2]

[2] These thinkers are among the many who have suggested that structural commonalities among languages are outweighed by the formative effect that lexicon and syntax have on cognition. As early as 1697, Leibniz asserted that language was not merely the means by which thought and experience were expressed, but was rather their "determining medium" (see Steiner 1975: 76); Wilhelm von Humbolt later argued, in the introduction to his translation of Aeschylus's *Agamemnon* (1816), that language generated a culturally specific *Weltansicht* or worldview. This is also what Wittgenstein was getting at when he declared, in the *Tractatus Logico-Philosophicus*, that "The limits of my language mean the limits of my world" (5.6), a notion also present in Borges's "La busca de Averroes" (1947) a story in which the eponymous philosopher—working from "the translation of a translation" of Aristotle's *Poetics*—struggles to understand the terms "comedy" and "tragedy" because he has no conceptual framework for staged drama. Around the same time, the work of Edward Sapir and his student Benjamin Lee Whorf was consolidated into the politically controversial Sapir-Whorf theory of linguistic relativity, to which explicit reference is made in *Arrival*. Taking the short step from there to the notion of untranslatability as such, in *A Linguistic Theory of Translation* (1965), J. C. Catford presented a model of untranslatability that, in addition to citing the major stumbling blocks of polysemy and phonetic play, presents the subtle qualitative differences between mundane referents (a bathroom, for example)—rather than philosophical keywords proposed by the *Dictionary of Untranslatables*—as the greatest challenges to translation.

First contact with the radical alterity of an extraterrestrial culture is an excellent foil for more mundane, but no less complex, questions of translation and its Others right here on our interconnected globe. The issues raised by the thinkers mentioned above returned to the humanistic limelight with the publication of Barbara Cassin's *Vocabulaire européen des philosophies, dictionnaire des intraduisibles* in 2004 [published in English as *The Dictionary of Untranslatables* in 2014].³ Cassin's compendium and its English counterpart have drawn significant attention not only for their detailed readings of a wide range of philosophical keywords—the "untranslatables" of the title—but also for the formulation of untranslatability on which the project is based.

Cassin situates her model of untranslatability between the twin precipices of logical universalism, prone to insensitivity toward the differences between languages and cultures, and of ontological nationalism, which essentializes and exoticizes those differences. The prize for navigating this narrow strip is the productive denaturalization (Cassin frames this as a Deleuzian "deterritorialization") of one's mother tongue (2016: 249). "Does one understand the same thing by 'mind' as by *Geist* or *esprit*," Cassin writes in her introduction to the *Dictionary*, "is *pravda* 'justice' or 'truth'?" (2014: xvii). Neither a search for equivalences among languages or a relinquishment of all hope of finding them, this refractive mode of reflection is, then, above all an exercise in constantly re-examining structures of meaning. The impossibility of mapping one language neatly onto another, moreover, is not the foreclosure of translation, in the sense of an absolute silence or linguistic lacuna; for Cassin, the untranslatables are a set of terms that *never stop* being translated, terms that "one keeps on (not) translating" (2014: xvii). In the language of global commerce, they are goods that never reach port.

It is—more or less—this formulation of untranslatability that Emily Apter adopts in her analysis of the circulation of cultural goods and

---

³ The translations in this volume and the addition of new material were under the editorial supervision of Jacques Lezra, Emily Apter, and Michael Wood. All future references will be to the English edition.

its discontents, *Against World Literature* (2013). Apter argues for understanding "the Untranslatable" (tellingly capitalized throughout)[4] "not as pure difference in opposition to the always translatable (rightly suspect as just another non-coeval form of the romantic Absolute, or fetish of the Other, or myth of hermeneutic inaccessibility) but as a linguistic form of *creative failure* with homeopathic uses" (20, my italics). Though the use of the word "failure" in the above quotation has generated debate for the way it seems to hold translation accountable for, as Lori Chamberlain put it years earlier, "crimes an original could not commit" (1988: 456), I will not address here how translation is policed, or by whom. The issue I would raise instead is that the use of the term "failure" seems to suggest that there can be some kind of translational "success" that offers an acceptable degree of equivalence: perhaps not a *perfect* translation, but one that is *good enough*. This kind of success would be dangerous indeed, in that it would forestall future reflection or revision and remove historical specificity from the linguistic and cultural considerations that go into translation and its analysis, when the reality is just the opposite: the connotation, even the denotation, of a word changes over time, occasionally over the course of just a few months. In the following pages, then, the term "translation failure" will be used only as it is by the contemporary writers discussed in this chapter: those instances in which a translator is not aware of, or cannot defend, a translational choice, or when the entire translational process collapses upon itself, generating not a series of versions but rather a monolithic silence.

Taking these formulations as a point of departure, I contend that we should think about untranslatability not in light of specific terms, works, or categories of discourse, but instead as integral to translation as a whole. Embracing the interpenetration of translation and

---

[4] Cassin asserts that the untranslatables should always be considered in the plural (2016: 243); Apter also utilizes Cassin's plural, lowercase formulation in *Against World Literature*, but her presentation of the Untranslatable as a category marked as a capitalized abstract noun reinforces the rift between translation and untranslatability—a rift that I propose we replace with a continuum.

untranslatability—without falling into the trap of nationalist ontologies—has the potential to shift our thinking in three ways. First, it would activate a practice of reading across languages and cultures attuned to the specificities of both the translated and translating languages. It would also recognize the series of active interventions behind even the most apparently straightforward cases of linguistic transfer and, as a result, would call into question the ownership of these works circulating globally as cultural goods. Finally, the multiplication of meaning that occurs when translation reveals itself not to be an even exchange of terms affords us new ways of thinking about general equivalents and equivalence, more generally. In the works of contemporary fiction studied in this chapter, failures of translation at the level of the cognate, the point where two languages would appear to offer the least resistance to—or to always already have completed—that process of transfer, allows for this understanding of untranslatability, not as being limited to individual terms or works, but rather as a productive and intrinsic facet of translation itself.

I. A Few Notes on (Un)Translation

Georges Mounin once asserted that "communication through translation can never be completely finished, which also demonstrates that it is never wholly impossible, either."[5] This paradoxical symbiosis between translation and untranslatability also marks an oft-cited passage from Derrida's *Monolingualism of the Other* (1996) that deals, at once precisely and obliquely, with the simultaneous un/translatability of everything and nothing. "Nothing is untranslatable," Derrida writes—in Patrick Mensah's translation,

> But the "untranslatable" remains—should remain, as my law tells me—
> the poetic economy of the idiom, the one that is important to me, for

---

[5] From *Les problèmes théoriques de la traduction* (Paris: Gallimard 1963) qtd. Bassnett 44.

I would die even more quickly without it, and which is important to me, myself to myself, where a given formal "quantity" always fails to restore the singular event of the original ... From the moment this economic equivalence—strictly impossible, by the way—is renounced, everything can be translated, but in a loose translation, in the loose sense of the word "translation" ... In a sense, nothing is untranslatable, but *in another* sense, everything is untranslatable; translation is another name for the impossible.

(1998: 76)

In Derrida's formulation, the untranslatable is first conceived as "l'économie poétique" (1996: 100)—that which is maintained or conserved in an irreducible form. The economic metaphor then shifts to stand in for linguistic commensurability: it becomes an exchange rate between signifying systems that allows for transfer with no remainder, "un mot pour un mot" (1996: 101). This *équivalence économique*— "strictly impossible" in Derrida's estimation, and undesirable for all the reasons outlined above—nonetheless resonates with the discussion of the circulation of cultural goods and the place of the subject in the dynamics of discursive power that attend it.

The axis of this shift between these two economies—one that closely guards meaning, one that offers it up to the market—is the slippage between importance and importation possible in the French verb *importer* but which is, ironically, lost in the English translation.[6] In the context of a work oriented specifically toward the politics of language and subject formation under its law, Derrida asserts that not only does the untranslatable *matter* (*importer*) to him, it can also be understood as that which *imports* (*importer*) him to himself; it is "qui

---

[6] Though it differs in emphasis and scope, this reading of the multiple valences of the verb *importer* is indebted to Jacques Lezra's in *Untranslating Machines* (2017). It bears mention also that the passage is presented differently on the physical space of the page: in the Gallimard edition, Derrida's ruminations on untranslatability are nearly eclipsed by a footnote that begins pages earlier and deals, among other things, with the internal fissures inherent to any "natural" language. In the Stanford University Press edition, this commentary is presented as an endnote. In both form and content, this note in the French edition reinforces Derrida's ruminations on the body text and forces a process of "loose translation" between them.

m'importe, moi-même à moi-même" (1996: 101). Embedded in this second meaning is the notion that language, and more precisely the untranslatable, has the capacity to denaturalize identity (the inverse, one could say, of the processes of subjective formation through language proposed by the linguistic relativists) in a process that divides, distances, and then presents one's self to oneself. While tied to the global market's language of importation, this dual formulation of economy is indeed *poetic*, in the sense of its being constructive: as we will see, this distancing movement contains within it the seed of both a political subject and a mode of reading.

Once the economy of equivalence is abandoned and translation is released to the loose translation of itself—"dans une traduction lâche au sens lâche du mot 'traduction'" (1996: 102)—the practice becomes at once *possible* and the complement, if not the synonym, of the untranslatable.[7] With these respective valorizations of iteration and approximation, both Derrida and Mounin present untranslatability as more than an illuminating exception to the rule of equivalence: it becomes the condition of possibility of translation itself, insofar as it asserts that it is the provisional nature of any translation that allows it to serve as a proxy for the original. Translation, in other words, is possible *precisely because* nothing is translatable. The concept of untranslatability thus becomes an essential part of what makes translation a vital (both important and dynamic) literary form. It also drives both translators and readers to consider the specific historical, social, and cultural conditions of the moment in which a work is created, at the same time it calls for new translations to be created in response to evolving linguistic sensibilities.

The perpetual reevaluation and renovation inherent to this formulation of (un)translatability is a prominent motif both in the contemporary Latin American fictions of translation here examined,

---

[7] The idea that translation and untranslatability are, in fact, one and the same is suggested by Paul de Man (with reference to Derrida's reading of "The Task of the Translator" in an imperfect French translation) in the final chapter of *The Resistance to Theory* (1986: 80).

and in their precursors. One notable case is the work of Juan José Saer, an Argentinean writer of Syrian descent whose temporary move to Paris at thirty ended up turning into a permanent relocation; a writer for whom questions of language and displacement are central, and a figure of no small importance to the novelists examined in this chapter. Saer's writing is marked by obsessive revision—both in terms of the precision of its prose and in its tendency to go back over phrases and ideas—clarifying, correcting, and expanding upon the story while often whittling away at the instrument of its telling. This is certainly the case in his 1969 novel *Cicatrices* [*Scars* trans. Steven Dolph 2011], inspired by the events surrounding a murder-suicide that took place several years earlier. In Saer's version, former union activist Luis Fiore has a very public fight with his wife on May Day and shoots her twice in the parking lot of a local bar, then kills himself during the investigation of his case. There is no question as to his guilt: *Cicatrices* is a novel that asks not *what* happened, but *how* it did, coiling back on itself in a series of divergent accounts, as each chapter brings the narrative one revolution closer to the crime that draws its narrative threads together.

Within this relativizing and fragmented novel, the vignette that frames Saer's narrative strategy and aligns it with the problem of translation centers on Ernesto López Garay, the judge assigned to the Fiore case. In the privacy of his chambers, Garay is obsessively translating Oscar Wilde's *The Picture of Dorian Gray*, his occupation and his avocation dovetailing on a metaphorical level at the point where the hermeneutics of evidentiary and linguistic analysis coincide. Saer's description of this activity foregrounds the play and misalignments between languages, the continuity between translation and untranslatability: for each word the judge looks up in the dictionary, a vertiginous array of synonyms and related lexical forms fans out before him. "I turn to the book and read," states Garay:

> Three o'clock struck, and four, and the half hour rang its double chime, but Dorian Gray did not stir. He was trying to gather up the scarlet threads of life, and to weave them into a pattern; to find his way through the sanguine labyrinth of passion through which he was wandering.

In red, I mark the word chime. The dictionary says, armonía; clave; juego de campanas; repique; sonar con armonía; repicar; concordar. Then I look up stir. It says, removerse; agitar; revolver; incitar; moverse; bullir; tumulto; turbulencia. I turn to T and look up threads. It says, hilo; fibra; enhebrar; atravesar.

I put down the green pen and pick up the black. I write, Dieron las tres y después las cuatro, y después la media hora hizo sonar su doble repique (teo) (campanada), pero Dorian Gray no se movió. Estaba tratando de reunir (juntar) (amontonar) (hilvanar) (enhebrar) (atravesar) los hilos (pedazos) (fragmentos) escarlatas (rojos) (rojizos) de su vida, y darles una forma, para hallar su camino a través del sanguíneo (sangriento) laberinto de pasión por el cual (que) había estado vagando.

(2011: 179)

Each step in the move from dictionary to translational draft adds new layers of complexity and divergence, ranging from a term's phonetic characteristics and register (repique/teo), to the image it generates (hilos/pedazos/fragmentos) or its degree of emphasis (escarlatas/rojos/rojizos). Both Saer's Spanish and Dolph's English juxtapose the two languages, the repetition within difference suggesting the impossibility of completing the transfer through the multiplication of translational alternatives. In this way, Saer presents us with a scarlet thread to follow through contemporary translation narratives, tracing the formulation of translation as a process of *opening up* meanings, rather than consolidating them within the limiting economy of equivalence.[8]

---

[8] A similar sense of linguistic vertigo marks Saer's *El entenado* (1982) [*The Witness* trans. Margaret Jull Costa 1990], though in this case the sense of estrangement arises within a single linguistic system. The novel centers on a young orphan who secures work aboard an ill-fated ship; when the crew is attacked by an indigenous tribe on the shores of the New World, the narrator is one of the few who are spared to learn how to live among them. Part of this process involves an intensive, and often perplexing, immersion in the "lengua imprevisible, contradictoria" (172) [unpredictable, contradictory language] of the tribe, and the interpretation of one term in particular: the pervasive "*def-ghi*," described repeatedly as "sonidos rápidos y chillones" (33) [fast, shrill sounds], reinforcing the impenetrability of the utterance. This radically foreign expression is, nonetheless, composed of profoundly familiar raw materials: six consecutive letters of the Roman alphabet. In this way, Saer defamiliarizes the linguistically mundane and insists on the otherness inherent to all language use.

II. Fragments of a Vessel

The notion that untranslatability is an intrinsic part of translation as a whole and not a subset of specific cases also underlies Walter Benjamin's seminal text "The Task of the Translator" (1923). In the essay, which served as the introduction to his translation of Baudelaire's *Tableaux Parisiens*, Benjamin addresses the question of translatability [*Übersetzbarkeit*], but he frames it according to the dual question of whether a given work will find the translator best suited to it, and whether it naturally "lends itself to translation" (2005: 254). Translatability, in the sense addressed here, makes its appearance shortly thereafter. In one of the many metaphors that add layers of translation to the essay in their own right, Benjamin suggests that all translations are untranslatable, due to the difference in the relationship between original and translation with respect to the language in which they are expressed. Whereas "content and language form a certain unity in the original, like a fruit and its skin," the language of a translation hangs loosely from its content, "like a royal robe with ample folds" (258). It is no coincidence, it seems, that in the title of these reflections on translation, "Die Aufgabe des Übersetzers," the term "Aufgabe" can mean both "task," as it is translated into English, and renunciation, the term serving as the "utterance and demonstration of a task at once possible and impossible," as Lisa Block de Behar so lucidly asserts (2003: 12). This relatively conservative metaphor appears, however, alongside reflections on the essential connection between translation and untranslatability grounded not in the relation between versions of a text, but rather in the relation between languages.

Anticipating Octavio Paz's observation in *Traducción: literatura y literalidad* (1971) ["Translation: Literature and Letters"] that "the sun praised in an Aztec poem is not the sun of the Egyptian hymn, although both speak of the same star" (1992: 153), Benjamin posits the problem of linguistic incommensurability by way of a most quotidian example: "In the words *Brot* and *pain*, what is meant is the same, but the way of meaning it is not. This difference in the way of meaning permits the word *Brot* to mean something other to a German than what the word *pain* means to a Frenchman, so that these words are not interchangeable for them" (2005: 257). Through the notion of the way of meaning (*Art des Meinens*), Benjamin illustrates the way translation brings the social and cultural nuances of a language into play with every word—one of the central premises of the model of untranslatability discussed above.⁹ Though the terms *Brot* and *pain* denote more or less the same substance, their connotations are radically different. This difference, of course, is often glossed over (rather than glossed) in the interest of expediency and in order for translation (and the myriad cultural and economic transactions that depend on it) to take place in the most efficient and uncomplicated way possible.

As demonstrated by the example of *Brot* and *pain* above, Benjamin's model of translation poses a challenge to even supposedly simple instances of interlinguistic transfer. The translator, he argues, should not aspire to the untenable aim of finding identical terms in the target language, because

> just as fragments of a vessel, in order to be articulated together, must follow one another in the smallest detail, but need not resemble one another, so, instead of making itself similar to the meaning [*Sinn*] of the original, the translation must rather, lovingly and in detail, in its own language, form itself according to the manner of meaning [*Art des Meinens*] of the original, to make both recognizable as the broken part of a greater language.
>
> (Jacobs 1975: 762)

I have cited Carol Jacobs' translation here because—as both Jacobs and Paul de Man have observed—Harry Zohn's version, by far the most widely used in English, diverges from the German on a key point: the translation of the term *folgen*. Whereas Jacobs stays close with her choice of "follow," Zohn opts for "match," effacing precisely that which makes Benjamin's proposal unique. Rather than understanding translation

---

⁹ This reading diverges slightly from that of Samuel Weber, who in *Benjamin's —abilities* takes a more structuralist approach to the notion of the *modus significandi* (2008: 71-2).

as metaphor—as its etymology would encourage—Benjamin's choice of the term *folgen* assumes no identity between the terms. De Man expands upon this point, asserting that what Benjamin is describing is "a metonymic, a successive pattern, in which things follow, rather than a metaphorical unifying pattern in which things *become one* by resemblance" (1986: 90, my italics).[10] This notion of metonymy in the context of translation—non-identical pieces combining to signal, though never fully recreate, the pure language of the *reine Sprache*—is central to understanding untranslatability as a condition and central feature of translation proper.

Among the many contemporary Latin American writers who engage translation on a thematic level in their work, one who incorporates the imagery of Benjamin's seminal essay in a strikingly explicit fashion is Pablo De Santis, whose *La traducción* [The translation] appeared in Argentina in 1998, the same year that saw the publication of two other translation narratives in that country, Salvador Benesdra's *El traductor* [The translator] and Néstor Ponce's *El intérprete* [The interpreter]. The novel is narrated by Miguel De Blast, a translator of Russian scientific texts who has been invited to attend a conference of his peers working across a range of languages and specializations in a deserted town at the end of the inhabited world aptly named Puerto Esfinge, after the Sphinx—that mythical creature who trafficked in metaphors and, through Oedipus, showed humankind an image of itself as it looks from a distance.

Underscoring, as *Borges e os orangotangos eternos* did, the resonances between the hermeneutic dimension of translation and detective work, the conference in *La traducción* takes a turn for the grisly with a rash of mysterious suicides that center, precisely, on "la lengua del Aqueronte" (1998: 161), a mythical pre-Babelian language

[10] According to de Man, interlinguistic transfer is further complicated by the fact that it is impossible to avoid reading through layers of associative interference. In de Man's reading, *Brot* evokes Hölderlin's *Brot und Wein*, then echoes back onto the French, which presents an entirely different connotation for *pain et vin*, cheapening the image. This complication extends in both directions in the construction of meaning: the presence of the sign in another language retroactively generates interference in the meaning of the first (1986: 87).

named after Charon, the ferryman of the River Styx. The language was studied by a small group of academics who believed the key to decoding it lay in in the string of incomprehensible words in Canto XXXI of Dante's *Inferno* uttered by Nemrod, the king who aspired to build the Tower of Babel and whose punishment was "to understand and be understood by no one" (162). The first to fall victim to this sacred language is an occultist who specializes in the Enochian utterances transmitted to John Dee in the late sixteenth century. As the deaths grow more numerous, it becomes clear that exposure to this "perfect language"—which is thought to grant eternal life to those who know but never speak it—is decidedly hazardous to one's health.

De Santis announces *La traducción*'s engagement of the tropes of translation theory early and often. The very first words of the novel, in fact, are:

> Tengo sobre mi escritorio un faro de cerámica. Me sirve como pisapapeles, pero es sobre todo una molestia. En el pie se lee *Recuerdo de Puerto Esfinge*. La superficie del faro está cubierta de estrías, porque ayer, al acomodar los originales de una traducción, el faro se cayó del escritorio. Con paciencia, uní los pedazos: quien haya intentado rearmar un jarrón roto, sabe que, por minucioso que sea su empeño, hay fragmentos que nunca aparecen.
>
> (1998: 11)

> I have a ceramic lighthouse on my desk. I use it as a paperweight, but it's mostly a nuisance. On its base are written the words *A Memento from Puerto Esfinge*. The surface of the lighthouse is covered in cracks because it fell from my desk yesterday when I moved the original of a text I was translating. I carefully joined the pieces: as anyone who has tried to put a broken vase back together knows, no matter how painstaking their efforts, there are fragments that never appear.[11]

---

[11] A note on this translation: in addition to the reading of "acomodar" that follows the corporality of the image of the lighthouse bears mention: it has a "foot" in Spanish, and its cracks are "estrías," which can be either "striations" or "stretch marks" (a very vivid image when thinking about translation and fecundity, as Benjamin does, and Derrida

Readers familiar with the myths and metaphors of translation will notice the density of references in this passage. The image of the shattered lighthouse—which, consolidating the confusion of the unfolding events, is later said to "echar oscuridad" (46) [cast darkness] rather than light—evokes the Tower of Babel and, with it, the *reine Sprache* that was lost when it fell. Furthermore, it is hard to ignore the echoes of "The Task of the Translator" in the image of the "jarrón roto" with which the narrator characterizes his difficulty in putting the shattered lighthouse back together. In this version of the foundational myth, however, the figure of an angry god exacting vengeance through the destruction of the tower is replaced by the pages of a source text— equally sacred, according to more conservative notions of translation. Given the resistance to translational equivalence embedded in these references to Benjamin (and, as we will see, elsewhere in the novel), De Santis's choice to have his translator protagonist's commemorative lighthouse-as-Tower-of-Babel break precisely in the act of "acomodar"—in Spanish, the verb means both "to accommodate" and "to place"—the original of a recent project, as though it were an excessive accommodation of, or adherence to, the original that causes the accident in the first place. Meanwhile, though the resonance between "pie" as the base of the souvenir and "pie" as the space on the printed page that is allotted to the translator's note is also lost in translation, the play on words connects the site of the object's inscription with this textual space.[12] Following this Benjaminian reading through, the final sentence of the novel's first paragraph can be said to posit the radical incommensurability of languages: not only are the pieces of the broken Gefäß/vessel/vase/vasija/jarrón not identical among themselves, they do not come back together to reconstitute the lost whole (though, even

after him). I chose the term "vase" because "jarrón" is fairly colloquial and—though the image certainly evokes Benjamin's metaphor—"vessel" seemed heavy-handed. The German "Gefäß" operates across several registers, from the almost Biblical "vessel" (Hans Christian Hagedorn, in the 1996 anthology *Teorías de la traducción* edited by Dámaso López García, opts for "vasija" [344]) to the mundane "pot" or "jug" and even "vase" (Langenscheidt).

[12] See Chapter 3 for more on the space of the footnote.

with gaps between them, they manage to suggest what was lost). This ill-fated memento from an ill-fated trip thus sets untranslatability at the very center of translational practice: De Santis not only integrates into his fiction Benjamin's translational metaphor of the broken vessel and the relationship of kinship (but not identity) between languages that the image suggests; in the hollows and scars that remain on the surface of the lighthouse, he also asserts the impossibility of arriving at any sort of antebabelian linguistic plenitude.

Impossibility, and also undesirability. The destruction of the Tower of Babel, while sometimes a nuisance—as anyone who has ever tried to navigate public transportation or buy a roll of toilet paper in a language completely unknown to them can attest—is ultimately presented as being aligned with life, with both a social and cultural vitality and, returning to Benjamin, an *after*life. In contrast, the antebabelian tongue—which, as the Edenic language in which all was originally named, eradicates the gaps between ways of meaning—is directly connected to the death of several characters, suggesting the grave consequences of the stasis produced by equivalence. This line of thinking is voiced most clearly by Puerto Esfinge's chief of police, who argues that it is precisely the pluralistic, contingent nature of language that stems from the gap between word and object (and therefore the distance between languages) that makes it worthwhile in the first place. In this novel that features a translator who becomes a detective of sorts, the police chief is an undercover philosopher of language, as well. When De Blast tells him that the deceased were all studying a language "anterior a la torre de Babel. El lenguaje en el que Adán nombró a las cosas. Una lengua perfecta" (1998: 141) [that predates the Tower of Babel. The language Adam used to name all things. A perfect tongue], the police chief replies, "Si tuviéramos que nombrar las cosas una sola vez, si bastara una palabra para aclararlo todo, la vida en este pueblo sería espantosa … ¿Sabe cuál es la única lengua perfecta? La que ayuda a matar el tiempo" (142) [If we only needed to name things once, if just one word were enough to explain everything, life in this town would be horrific … You know what the perfect language is? The one that helps you kill time]. The assertion is grounded in the notion that language is inherently, and fortuitously, plural. Picking up the (scarlet) thread of Saer's description of translation, I would argue that the same incommensurable nuances within and between languages not only define translation as a vital, evolving process, they also offer a means of writing and reading rooted in specificity and variability, over and against the extractive convenience of unexamined linguistic transfer.

III. The Problem with False Friends

The interpenetration of translation and untranslatability—the notion that the infinite iterations, contextualization, and relativization of meaning associated with the untranslatable is not a limit case, but rather an essential part of translation itself—brings us to the cognate and its mobilization in two works of contemporary Latin American fiction: Salvador Benesdra's *El traductor* [The translator] and Alan Pauls's *El pasado* [*The Past* trans. Nick Caistor 2007]. Through an analysis of the way these two texts thematize translation failure at the point where translation appears not only most possible, but indeed hardly necessary, I will argue for the integration of untranslatability into the production and reading of translations as a movement toward what Gayatri Chakravorty Spivak has described as a planetary understanding of culture, a valorization of specificity and complexity over and against the homogenizing sweep of globalization and the efficient rendering of cultural materials upon which it depends.

Though virtually unstudied in this context, the cognate is a critical element in thinking about translation and its close kinship with untranslatability. Kinship in the Benjaminian sense, as well: cognates may be born-together, etymologically speaking, but—as we will see—they are hardly identical twins. Often relied upon as a teaching tool in second language acquisition, the cognate presents a series of linguistic pitfalls and roadblocks that can threaten both translation and interpersonal communication when orthographic and phonetic similarity conceal significant variance in the meaning of two terms.[13] These cases of illusory affinity, first assigned the iconic appellation of "faux amis" by Maxime Koessler in 1926, complicate the interlingual transfer of cultural goods and thus have far-reaching implications for the global market and the discursive hierarchies that attend it.

Ricardo Zevi, the translator protagonist of Salvador Benesdra's *El traductor*, published posthumously in 1998, is no stranger to the dynamics of globalized culture. When Turba—the small, left-leaning publishing house that employs him as a salaried translator—is absorbed by a large, politically conservative international media conglomerate, Zevi's work is outsourced to less experienced employees chosen by the corporation. In a conceit that evokes not only the translator's status within the literary cultural field, but also that of the "peripheral" market in which Zevi plies his trade, our protagonist is pushed further and further toward the margins of Turba's activities.[14] The effects of this merger, and indeed the broader economic trends that subtend it in both the novel and its historical context—namely, the presidency of Carlos Menem (1989-99), during which large-scale privatization and foreign investment shaped the country's economic and cultural landscape—are central elements in the narrative.[15]

Despite Zevi's frustration at his professional situation, when a new translator named Celeste—a name that evokes the colors of Argentina's

---

[13] For more on cognates in the language classroom and even homophony within the same language system, see Chacón Beltrán 2006 and Roca Varela 2011.
[14] The ways in which this marginality is addressed in the representation of the physical spaces occupied by Zevi are explored in the chapter "Writing off the Map." The publishing landscape in Argentina in the years following the economic crisis is outlined by Graciela Adamo in Allen (2007: 53-8).
[15] Denise Kripper offers a rich account of the novel's engagement with this historico-political moment in "Los agentes de la traducción: las ficciones del traductor como relatos de mercado" (2017).

national flag, known as the *blanquiceleste* [white and sky blue]—is brought in, he attempts to establish rapport with her, offering advice on the most common pitfalls of their profession: that of succumbing to what Granger and Swallow have called "the fatal attraction of the cognate" (1988: 114). "Están todas las trampas de la falsa similitud" [You've got all the traps of false similarity], Zevi says,

> que entre lenguas romances son fatales. ¿Sabes cuántas chantas traducen el *pois não* brasileño por pues no, aunque es exactamente el contrario, o el *stare stanco* italiano por estar estancado, en lugar de cansado? En francés tenés de estas trampas a carradas. Te juro que en una novela he leído cómo un personaje se apoyaba sobre su 'orejero' en lugar de su almohada, porque el tipo que lo tradujo se consideró suficientemente intuitivo para no necesitar consultar *oreiller* en un diccionario.
>
> (323)

> Between Romance languages, they're deadly. Do you know how many hacks translate the Brazilian *pois não* as *pues no*, even though they're complete opposites? Or the Italian *stare stanco* as being blocked, *estancado*, rather than tired? French has these traps by the boatload. I swear, I read a novel once where a character leaned back on their wing chair instead of their pillow because the guy who translated it figured that *oreiller* was so intuitive he didn't need to look it up in the dictionary.

Returning to the fraught category of "translation failure," it does seem appropriate to use the term here, in the sense that these errors are genuine mistakes and fail to push us toward reconsiderations or recontextualizations.[16] The translator simply hits a false note and keeps playing, keeping time with the feverish pace of production even as the product itself is devalued by this expediency.

Shortly thereafter, when Celeste is promoted past him at Turba, Zevi bitterly returns to the topic of false cognates—not as a means

---

[16] Beyond etymological considerations, which can also be quite interesting.

of establishing professional solidarity, but rather as an emblem of everything that is wrong with the publishing industry, the intellectual goods it produces, and the minds these texts both depend upon and shape. "Por fin entendía," writes Benesdra, "cómo en un país donde hay un conocimiento masivo de las lenguas extranjeras podían todavía—y por épocas cada vez más—editarse libros donde *bagnole* no era auto sino bañadera" (356) [I finally understood how in a country where so many people speak foreign languages, they could still publish books—more and more at certain moments—that have *bagnole* as a bathtub, not a car]. The problem with translation in Argentina, then, is the publishing industry itself, insofar as it is increasingly governed by the mandate of expediency established when a multinational media conglomerate takes over. Though the nation has plenty of individuals capable of producing better translations, corporate pressure to produce efficiently, coupled with a general sense of indifference, leads to incomplete and irresponsible translations. Celeste is simply the icon, or flag-bearer, of the sweep of globalization.

In addition to his critique of the cultural impact of global capitalism, Benesdra posits that the danger in this particular form of expediency, as before, is one of over-identification, of imagining similarities between linguistic and cultural systems where none exist and, in the process, collapsing the singularity of each—an obvious culturally imperialist gesture. Translation failure is, in this case, not only a linguistic, but also a political matter. What is needed is *inefficiency*, reflection; the recognition of distance. Ultimately, beyond the challenges these misleading cognates or "false friends" present to the translator on a technical or linguistic level, they also testify to the irreducibility of these systems over and against the illusion of smooth intercultural transfer— "the imposition of the same system of exchange everywhere," as Spivak describes it in *Death of a Discipline* (2003: 72)—that is the hallmark of globalization. There is also a clear parallel to be drawn between the assumption of equivalence based on superficial similarity and the imperialist tendency toward what Lawrence Venuti has described as "domestication," that is, the attempt to make the translation seem a natural part of the target language literary system.[17] Much like the systemic institutional pressures described by Venuti, which manifest predominantly as an editorial and critical imperative to render foreign texts in accordance with the target culture's aesthetic and ideological landscape, the (often unconscious) conflation of terms across languages inevitably, violently, forces the source language to mold itself to the target language, rather than the other way around. Benesdra's novel alerts us to the aesthetic, and indeed the political, risks inherent to this excessive identification.

IV. The Problem with True Friends

Though the encounter with false cognates in Benesdra's novel provides a vivid cautionary tale about the pitfalls of expediency and the darker side of a globalized publishing industry (of globalization in general), there is nothing particularly surprising about the scenes presented above. As I mentioned earlier, false cognates have been widely studied as linguistic traps; it is not much of a conceptual leap to assert that they pose a difficulty for the circulation of texts across languages. Yet whereas Benesdra's translator protagonist fixates on what might be described as an excessive confidence in translatability grounded in carelessness, Alan Pauls's depiction of translation failure in *El pasado* posits a radical notion of non-equivalence through a translational caesura reminiscent of Michael Cronin's notion of "blockage"—that

---

[17] Though I wholeheartedly agree with Venuti regarding the violence inherent to making translations into English conform to local (always ideologically inflected) norms, I do not personally advocate the introduction of a sense of foreignness into the text, even as I recognize that what it means to "introduce" a sense of "foreignness" is subjective and will vary from text to text. Instead of foreignizing the text according to criteria that are, necessarily, inflected by the translator's subjective situatedness and the cultural assumptions that attend it, I propose dividing the responsibility of anti-domestication between the reader and the translator (both of whom must consistently confront their own situatedness) through what I am calling a practice of distancing reading. For a potent indictment of editorial domestication, see Don Mee Choi's translator's note to *All the Garbage of the World, Unite!* (2011).

moment in which the "word or the expression or the equivalent allusion will not come, the textual whole does not seem the right fit and try as you might, there seems to be no way out, the words refuse to come to your rescue" (2003: 93). While for Cronin this blockage is a common experience for translators and has more to do with memory failure than incommensurability, the case of Pauls's translator protagonist is striking because it centers on a *true* cognate, if such a thing can be said to exist. As a result, Pauls's novel calls into question an entire way of thinking about linguistic transfer and the circulation of ideas and cultural objects.[18]

In *El pasado*, a young translator named Rímini—whose star is on the rise despite the self-destructive habits he energetically embraces after separating from his long-time girlfriend, Sofía—is hired to interpret for Jacques Derrida, who is passing through Buenos Aires to give a lecture at one of the city's many theaters.[19] The event goes brilliantly until Derrida decides to tell an anecdote about a Kafkaesque experience he once had involving the Czech police force, a suitcase, and an accusation of drug trafficking. Rímini, unable to call up the word *valija*—the most common term in Argentine Spanish for the object described, and almost phonetically identical to the French *valise*—suffers a breakdown on the stage, bringing his promising career to an abrupt end (or at least ushering in a traumatic sabbatical). The scene unfolds as follows:

> Al oír la palabra *valise* Rímini sintió otra vez el crujido del Coliseo, tuvo la impresión de que una fuerza extraña lo alejaba de todo y la voz del filósofo, hasta entonces diáfana como un cristal, se le volvió completamente impenetrable. No pudo seguir. Forcejeó con el filósofo larga, interminablemente, tratando de que admitiera que *valise* era otro de los inspirados neologismos en los que se especializaba, y cuando

---

[18] For a detailed reading of the novel and its relation to Argentinean history, see Gaspar (2014: 81–116).

[19] Translation is a recurring theme in the fiction of Alan Pauls, who—like nearly all the authors of this corpus—has also published a meaningful body of work as a translator. In addition to *Historia del pelo* (2010), mentioned below, the plot of his 1994 novel *Wasabi* involves the publication of the young narrator's novel in French.

el filósofo decidía soslayar la interrupción y siguió adelante con la conferencia, Rímini se encontró perdido en un bosque de sonidos misteriosos y lanzó un débil grito de pánico.

(Pauls 2003: 236)

when he came to the word *valise* Rimini suddenly experienced the same dry crack as at the Coliseo, felt as though a strange force was pushing him away from everything, and the philosopher's voice, which until then had been crystal clear, became completely impenetrable. He could not go on. He struggled long and hard to get the philosopher to admit that *valise* was another of the inspired neologisms he specialized in, and when Derrida decided to cut short the interruption and get on with his talk, Rimini was lost in a forest of mysterious sounds. He gave a weak yelp of panic.

(Pauls 2007: 201)

Rímini's experience pushes Cronin's notion of "translator's block" from an innocuous, if inconvenient, lack of words toward what Beverly Curran describes as a "pained silence or stutter" (2007: 236) that registers not only a linguistic impasse, but also the "effects of history" that mark the translator's tongue.

In contrast to the litanies drawn from Benesdra's *El traductor* about the perils of false cognates, in this case it is a pair of terms generally considered to be "true" cognates that sparks this breakdown of linguistic transfer (and, indeed, of the translator himself). Rímini's experience resonates with Michael Wood's description of the vast distances between the homonymic French and English versions of *justice* that he encountered while translating the term for the *Dictionary of Untranslatables*, all the more confounding because, in addition to looking and sounding the same, the two terms would appear to refer to an idea that "has or ought to have its counterpart in any language we can imagine" (2014: np).[20] In neither case do homophony (or near homophony) and symbolic approximation add up to equivalence.

---

[20] This assertion, which contradicts Catford's notion of philosophical universality, appears in Apter's introduction to the *Dictionary of Untranslatables* and in a brief text written by Wood for *The Huffington Post*.

Through its many references to the canon of translation theory, including but not limited to Derrida's role in this pivotal scene, the novel presents linguistic equivalence as fundamentally untenable, a desire for unity that is endlessly deferred. Fittingly, then, Benjamin's theory of linguistic and cultural transfer is also present. In its references to impermeability and, of course, in the image of the "forest of mysterious sounds," Pauls's description also evokes the metaphor of the "language forest" that Benjamin uses to describe—in topographical terms—the difference between an original and its translation. The latter, Benjamin claims, "finds itself not in the center of the language forest but on the outside facing the wooded ridge; it calls into it without entering, aiming at that single spot where the echo is able to give, it its own language, the reverberation of the work in the alien one" (2005: 258–9). Through this metaphor, we return to the notion of the metonymic quality of translation in Benjamin's formulation (and, indeed, the foundation for his famous translative *Nachleben*), though the idea is cast more subtly this time: from an external point, the translation is aimed at a dense tangle of multivalent terms, each imbued with a set of culturally determined connotations that, if laid out on the page, would look much like the annotated jumble of Wilde that Saer spreads across Ernesto Garay's desk. The translation, however, will only be able to resonate with one, or possibly two, of these meanings, which means that the echo that comes out will never match the sound that went in. The benefit of the loss implied in this arrangement is, for Benjamin, the rebirth of the work in a new historical, cultural, and linguistic context and, subsequently, the possibility this translational partiality creates for future iterations; all of which will be likewise incomplete, and all of which will draw attention to this incompleteness by forming part of a constellation of texts oriented toward, but never reaching, the linguistic unity of the *reine Sprache*.[21]

---

[21] Again, according to de Man, the *Wehen* of this rebirth should be understood just as much in terms of death as life. De Man observes that Benjamin "constantly uses" the term *überleben*, which he defines as living beyond one's own death. "The translation," he continues, "belongs not to the life of the original, the original is already dead, but the translation belongs to the afterlife of the original, thus assuming and confirming the death of the original" (1986: 85).

A different moment in the limelight, read through Jacques Lezra's analysis of homophony in *A Midsummer Night's Dream* and a later novel by Pauls in which Shakespeare's play figures prominently, offers insight into Rímini's translational blockage. Given the insistence on translation in *A Midsummer Night's Dream*, it is no surprise that it should appear in narratives that mobilize the practice thematically.[22] One particularly memorable scene comes at the start of the play's third act, for example, when we find Bottom and Quince in the midst of translating (what today we might call localizing) those disturbing "things in this comedy of Pyramus and Thisby that will never please" (III.i 8–9)—namely, death and lions—into something more palatable by adding prologue upon prologue that insist on the play-within-a-play's status as a play, imposing layers of *unreality* onto their imagined audience's willingly suspended disbelief. Bottom exits, followed by Puck, and returns "translated" (in the words of Quince), bearing the head of an ass.

One of the first things the reader of Pauls's *Historia del pelo* (2010) learns about the novel's protagonist is that, during his employ with a small municipal stage company, he is asked to translate the play. Moreover, he is asked to recreate Bottom and Quince's original translational gesture by replacing those things that "will never please" the troupe's adolescent audience—in this case, the "haughty verses" of the original—with "la fruta abrillantada de siempre, chistecitos, referencias a la actualidad local, canciones ridículas" (2010: 11) [the same old shiny fruit, little jokes, local references, silly songs]. Not a series of prologues, then, but a similar gesture of localization aimed at appeasing an imagined public. In both *El pasado* and *Historia del pelo*, Pauls's invocation of the stage highlights the tension between the private "trance" his translator

---

[22] Another example is the delightful film by Argentinean director Matías Piñeiro, *Hermia & Helena* (2017), the protagonist of which travels to New York City for a residency to translate *A Midsummer Night's Dream* into Spanish, though she spends as much time translating herself in this new context as she does working on the play.

protagonists enter when they work, and its very public end product, whether a book in circulation or a public event or performance. It also points to the artificial, slippery nature of language—a subject central to Shakespeare's play, as well.

Back in the enchanted wood (another forest of language), when his fellow performers flee at the sight of him, Bottom accuses them of trying to frighten or "make an ass" of him (III.i 105) and breaks into song to announce their failure (or to manage his fear). In this song, Bottom runs through a litany of birds before alighting on the cuckoo—the source of many terms in English, including "cuckold," for their practice of laying eggs in the nests of others—"Whose note full many a man doth mark, / and dares not answer nay" (III.i 119–20). As Lezra reads the scene:

> A man "dare not" "neigh," because he understands a "neigh," whatever it may designate in Ass, to be uttered *in Ass*, and to designate collectively the natural language I am calling, rudely and mechanically, Ass. To answer "nay" is to "neigh," or to be an Ass: the "neigh-ness" of "neigh" removes "nay" from the language human animals can use without losing their humanity, in whole or—like Bottom—in part.
>
> (2012: 7)

Indeed, were Bottom to be called by the cuckoo, to answer "nay" would mean being doubly an ass: first, in the denial of an infidelity announced, and second, by inhabiting a moment of homophonic interference that destabilizes the language in which he speaks.

Once translated into a hybrid being, Bottom's "nay" becomes an echo at once different and indistinguishable from a "neigh" in his other (unacknowledged) tongue; much of the humor of the scene rests on these double entendres, this string of translations—physical, unwitting, and otherwise. To complicate matters further, the neigh-nay homonym could be understood as what Granger and Swallow call a "partially deceptive" cognate, that is, a set of terms that semantically overlap with and differ from their homonymic counterparts, and which are, therefore, "undoubtedly more treacherous" than completely false cognates (1988: 109). That is, the "neigh" expressed in Ass—which could also be a human "nay"—could mean either a "nay" in Ass, or anything else in that language. The two terms overlap but do not coincide across their different ways of meaning.

The accidental kinship generated by homophony thus contains its own translational blockage or stutter: precisely because the utterance exists in both Human and Ass—and because it represents a point at which the two are impossible to differentiate, given the original oral presentation of the play—it produces its own interference, rendering itself an *unspeakable* node within language, not unlike the one described by Michel Serres in his analysis of the term *hôte*. According to Serres, the linguistic remainder by which the term's dual meaning complicates the relation between guest and host, creates one of many "black spots in language" in which it is impossible to distinguish not only meaning, but directionality, conflating sender and receiver (2007: 16). In Serres's example, moreover, it is not only the denotations and connotations of superficially similar terms that prove unwieldy, masking a vast chasm of cultural difference; it is also a question of semantic proliferation even within a single language, a plurality of referents that threaten to crash the economy of signification.

This simultaneous multiplication and evacuation of meaning becomes a symbolic refrain in *El pasado*, beginning with the *valise-valija* episode. Throughout the rest of the novel, bags are almost invariably depicted as overflowing, tearing, or opening up at the seams. Not long after the incident that Rímini and his girlfriend Carmen call his "precoz Alzheimer lingüístico" (2003: 282) [early-onset linguistic Alzheimer's], Rímini has a second panic attack during one of his rare outings. After lunch one afternoon, the couple decides to see a movie downtown. When a technical glitch eliminates the subtitles midway through, Rímini notices that not only has he been watching a French film, but also—to his dismay—that he is unable to follow the dialogue, though up until just recently he'd made a living translating the language:

Supo entonces que todo lo que había entendido hasta ese momento lo había entendido gracias al subtitulado. Sin él, a solas con las voces que hablaban, que seguían hablando en francés, Rímini descubría que la lengua ya no le decía absolutamente nada … Rímini miró a Carmen. Su cara impasible lo desesperó. "¿Cómo … ?" Era obvio. Carmen entendía sin necesidad de leer. El huérfano era él; él, sólo él, era el que lo perdía todo. Se levantó, eludió unas rodillas, una *valija* abierta, un paraguas, corrió por el pasillo … y diez segundos después, abrazado a su hijo dormido, lloraba a gritos en uno de los compartimientos del baño.

(Pauls 2003: 285, my italics)

He realized that everything he had understood up to that point had been thanks to the subtitles. Without them, left only with the voices that were still speaking French, Rimini discovered the language meant absolutely nothing to him … Rimini looked at Carmen. Her tranquil face left him in despair. "How … ?" The answer was obvious: Carmen could understand without having to read. He was the orphaned one; he and only he was losing everything. He got up, pushed past knees, an open case [*valija*], an umbrella, ran up the aisle … and ten seconds later, clinging to his still sleeping son, he was howling in one of the cubicles of the men's toilets.

(Pauls 2007: 242–3)

No stranger to the visual language of film, Pauls inserts a cameo in his protagonist's retreat from the site of his second linguistic humiliation; the reader, having just been reminded of the cause of Rímini's consternation, cannot help but catch the reference of the valise, open like a wound on the floor of the theater.[23] Having established this allusion, Pauls repeats it over the course of the novel, with variations. Most notable among these are the image of Ida, the current lover of Sofía's father, trying to wrestle a riding crop and a few leather accessories back into the *valija* she drops in her flight from Rímini's shouted greeting (2003: 473) and that of the young protagonist himself, who, having

---

[23] Pauls has also written an extensive corpus of film criticism and scripts for film and television.

begun his life as a translator at an early age, is described as carrying "una valija desbordante de libros" (2003: 489), that same *valise* again, this time *overflowing* with books. In the context of our present discussion of untranslatability and the metonymic conception of language, these images suggest an excess inherent to language precisely at the *inarticulation*—both the failure to speak and the failure to join—of *valise* and *valija*, the referent itself a symbol travel and transfer, but also one of containment. (One, moreover, in which we hear echoes of Benjamin's legendary flight across the Pyrenees with drafts of the *Passagenwerk* in his suitcase.) At these moments, more explicitly than perhaps anywhere else in the novel, the narrative of translation failure draws attention to a linguistic equation that will always have a remainder, an untranslatable and unassimilable balance.

The metaphorical pivot of Derrida's reflections on the untranslatable cited above—the economic as both a limiting factor that preserves expressive specificity and a system that traffics in equivalences—reappears in the circulation of intellectual goods across cultural and linguistic borders.[24] In these novels by Salvador Benesdra and Alan Pauls, the translational failures that attend the cognate complicate

---

[24] The connection between translation and debt appears in the fictions, as well: Rímini feels it in *El pasado*, locked in his room every Sunday feverishly translating away.

El simple hecho de que algo estuviera escrito en otra lengua, una lengua que él conocía pero no su lengua materna, bastaba para despertar la idea ... de que ese libro, artículo, relato o poema estaba *en deuda*, debía algo inmenso, imposible de calcular y por lo tanto, naturalmente, de pagar, y que él, Rímini, el traductor, era quien tenía que hacerse cargo de la deuda *traduciendo*. (2003: 107, emphasis in the original)

The simple fact that something was written in another language, one that he knew but which was not his mother tongue, was sufficient to awaken in him the idea ... that this book, article, short story or poem was somehow in debt, a debt so huge it was incalculable and therefore impossible to repay but which he, Rímini, the translator, had to take responsibility for by translating. (2007: 85, no emphasis)

Spivak, for her part, conceives of this translational "*Schuldigsein*" as being a debt to the mother tongue, "the language in which we are 'responsible'" (2012: 243). The intersection of debt and guilt in the German "Schuld" is particularly interesting in the context of translation: for the way Rímini feels compelled to translate, for the sense—via Benjamin—that the original always already contains the seed of its translation, for the notion of cultural responsibility embedded in discussions of translational ethics, and for Lori Chamberlain's assertion, mentioned earlier that translations are often held guilty for crimes an original could not commit.

two distinct but interrelated transactions: Benesdra's victims of false cognates end up selling shoddy wares to the readers of the target-language work, while Pauls's Rímini devalues the discourse he is hawking when he disrupts the illusion that Derrida's address was being unproblematically relayed from the start. Despite the thematic similarity between the two scenes, however, there is an important difference between them. While Benesdra's discussion of false cognates cautions against an overly credulous approach to phonetic resemblance, the motif of the *valija* in *El pasado* pushes the assumption of equivalence to its limit by insisting on the incommensurability of two terms that are almost identical in form, etymology, *and* referent—a gesture that demands a reconsideration of the dynamics of interlinguistic transfer as a whole.

V. Best Enemies

In the novels of Alan Pauls and Salvador Benesdra, the cognate—revealed to be false, even when "true"—emerges as a talisman of the structural presence of untranslatability. The linguistic incommensurability suggested by Pablo De Santis's "jarrón roto" asserts itself even in those instances when equivalence seems most tenable: homonyms that ostensibly refer to the same object. But what, precisely, is at stake in establishing continuity between translation and untranslatability by way of the relation between the homonymic "false friend" and those terms considered to be faithful cognates?

In *The Politics of Friendship* (1994), Derrida reads the construction of the political subject through an exploration of the concept of friendship in the writings of Schmitt, Nietzsche, Aristotle, and Montaigne. Over the course of his reflections, he insists time and again that the means of circumventing, or writing away from, the *old* name of democracy and its entrenched hierarchies is the defense of the singularity of the friend, the defense of his countability as a political subject. As such, his refrain of "how many?" not only refers to the notion, drawn from Aristotle, that to have too many friends is to have none—it is also the consistent reassertion of a multiplicity shored up by singularity.

This appreciation of the other as such is achieved, paradoxically, by aligning the figure of the true friend with that of the enemy. In Derrida's reading of Nietzsche, routed through Blake, the best or truest friend is the one who inhabits the position of the enemy, maintaining distance instead of allowing their subjectivities to collapse into one. "The true enemy," he writes, "is a better friend than the friend" even when waging war, because he will "hear what my name should, even if it does not, properly name: the irreplaceable singularity which bears it" (2005: 72). The good enemy produces or protects the distance required for the cultivation of respect—in scopic terms, the possibility of perspective—which in turn creates the conditions necessary for "a friendship without presence, without resemblance, without affinity, *without analogy*" (2005: 155, my italics). In the context of translation, this form of friendship would be one in which the differences between Benesdra's *pois não* and *pues no* were recognized and defended, along with the particularities of each phrase's usage in its respective language system.

Taking into account Rímini's primal scene of linguistic incommensurability, we see the "falsehood" embedded in even the "true" cognate. What is more, this productive form of enmity was there all along, born-together, embedded in the structure of its twinning. As Derrida observes, the enemy "did not *rise up*; he did not come *after* the friend to oppose or negate him. He was already there, this fellow creature, this double or this twin" (2005: 172).[25] As such, the linguistic figure serves as the "true enemy" described above, forcing

---

[25] The echo, here, of Don Mee Choi's *Translation is a Mode = Translation is an Antineocolonial Mode*: "As you may know, the first half of the title is from Harry Zohn's translation of 'The Task of the Translator' by Walter Benjamin. The other half, I hope, is its twin—a retranslation, a radical hybrid of Benjamin's brilliant concept and an antineocolonial stance ... I come from such twoness. I speak as a twin" (2020: 1).

a consideration of the processes of translation and localization upon which the transfer of cultural goods depends—and, by extension, of the geopolitical relations that determine the relative worth of these goods, the terms under which they can be consumed, the ways in which they are discussed, and so on.

The interpenetration of translation and untranslatability is, then, aligned with an ethics of reading. "In this era of global capital triumphant," Spivak writes in *Death of a Discipline*, "to keep responsibility alive in the reading and teaching of the textual is at first slightly impractical … The planet is, here, as perhaps always, a catachresis for inscribing collective responsibility as right" (2003: 102). This responsibility can be understood, through the figure of the true enemy, as the possibility of response, a response-ability that exists only insofar as there are two (or more) discrete, non-analogous, entities to make and answer the call.[26] In fact, Spivak herself draws a connection to *The Politics of Friendship* in her use of the term teleopoiesis, which can be understood not only as a form of making across distance, but also as *a making of* precisely the kind of distance necessary to the establishment of political subjectivity.[27]

This distance, in turn, generates a *distancing* mode of reading that—in contrast to Franco Moretti's polemical and ultimately unsatisfying strategy of *distant* reading, which analyzes national literatures according to the statistical coincidence of terms and tropes while giving little thought to questions of translation—privileges multiplicity and complexity over and against expediency. It reminds us that translation

---

[26] According to Derrida, "There is no respect, as its name connotes, without the vision and distance of a *spacing*," just as there can be "no responsibility without response" (2005: 252). The rejection of the analogous, here, also resonates with the earlier discussion of the metonymic, rather than metaphoric, relationship between translating terms, the pieces of the vessel that *follow*, rather than *match*, one another.

[27] Scheiner 2005 offers an account of Spivak's adaptation of this term from Derrida's use of *teleiopoiesis* in *The Politics of Friendship*.

is possible both despite and as a result of its impossibility and ushers us toward reading practices wary of the "successful" translation, which examine critically the way texts enter a target language system and posit the literary world-system as a planetary network of ever-shifting heterocosms that interact, nourish, and challenge—but are not reducible to, or exchangeable for—one another. The echo returns from the enchanted wood, insistent on the question: How many?

3
Writing in the Margins

Pies: pasos que en sus saltos dejan huellas en el cuerpo del texto. Patología: margen que el traductor comparte con otros desterrados ... que abre la polifonía.

Liliana Feierstein, "N de la T: los pies del texto"

My novels are hard to interpret; I think they often refuse interpretation. Though if there is one somewhat coherent thing about them, it might be in their form and not their content.

Mario Bellatin, interview with Gabriela Wiener

Mario Bellatin is an artist of the im-proper. From an "illustrated biography" of Yukio Mishima that traces the author's literary production and international travels in the years following his ritual suicide, to a controversial musical adaptation of his text *Bola negra* [Black ball] set in Ciudad Juárez, Bellatin's body of work offers a sustained, often transgressive, challenge to both intellectual property and generally held notions of propriety.[1] In a 2016 interview with *City of Asylum*, Bellatin

---

[1] Ciudad Juárez is a city on the border with the United States that has, especially in the years following the signing of the NAFTA treaty, been plagued by violence, particularly in the form of feminicides and human trafficking. The city has been described by Rita Segato as both "emblematic of women's suffering" and as "an emblematic place of economic globalization and neoliberalism, with its insatiable hunger for profit" (2010: 70). In an interview with Alice Driver, Bellatin first describes the project in terms of its impropriety, "I asked myself what should not be made about Ciudad Juárez, and I said, 'That's what I'm going to do'" (2013: 105). He then articulates a more nuanced approach in line with Segato's observation about the capitalist underpinnings of the human suffering in the city, asserting that "In spite of what we have seen in some images, there is an order to everything, an organization—everything is planned. Someone always benefits from the situation, except for the victims" (Driver 2013: 105).

summed up the first part of this challenge when he described the artist as an "antenna" through which a work passes such that the product of this transmission ultimately "belongs to everyone."[2]

This idea that ownership over texts is both collective and ephemeral underlies Bellatin's 2003 project the *Congreso de Dobles* [Conference of doubles]. An experiment to see just how dead the Author really is, the event was announced as a multi-day series of lectures at which four prominent Mexican writers—Margo Glantz, Salvador Elizondo, Sergio Pitol, and José Agustín—would present their work. What Bellatin delivered instead was a line of tables populated by stand-ins or "representatives" who had been trained by the authors in advance of the event to answer questions about their most famous works. Bellatin set up four small tables with two chairs facing one another at each. On each table was a microphone and a menu of topics created by each author, to which each stand-in had been trained to respond with specific remarks. As Bellatin describes it, the texts were offered to individual members of the audience in a "personal" way, face to face, "but the voices of the representatives are amplified and can be heard, simultaneously, throughout the room." These voices are joined by that of a translator "trying to attend to all four tables at once" (2003: 4).

The engineered chaos of this scene is not limited to replacing the invited authors by trained stand-ins: outside the immediate exchange between the audience member and the surrogate that takes place at each of the four simultaneously intimate and institutionally sterile tables, the conversations are amplified and layered over one another, creating a wall of sound that further abstracts and muddles the texts prepared by the authors listed in the program. The introduction of the translator, who represents the node at which these multiple voices convene as

---

[2] Though a far more extensive body of criticism exists in Spanish, several articles in English discuss Bellatin's ludic and disruptive approach to the literary establishment. Among these are Graciela Mochkofsky's article on the author's legal battle with the publishing house Tusquets, a profile for *The New York Times* by Larry Rohter, an academic article about *El jardín de la señora Murakami* by Emily Hind, and a piece on *Bola Negra: Ciudad Juárez, The Musical* by Alice Driver. See also review essays on English translations of his work written by Matt Bucher and myself; all references are listed in the bibliography.

he attends to all four tables at once, lays yet another veil of confusion over the proceedings. Even if the audience were willing to ignore the mediating agency of the surrogates and accept them as unproblematic mouthpieces, in the tumult it becomes impossible to identify the origin of the comments being made, ultimately diffusing the author's "voice" (read: fetishized "aura") to the point of its dissolution.

Bellatin's sustained challenge to the discursive privilege of the author, however, is not limited to other writers. His own authorial persona is a frequent subject of his dismantlings—among other things, he has been known to generate contradictory autobiographies and literary mythologies. The question of who, exactly, *Mario Bellatin* is—and what, exactly, he does—was taken up not long after the *Congreso* by Alan Pauls, who wrote:

> Me cuesta imaginar a Mario Bellatin como un escritor. Hace algunos años que no hago más que leerlo, que todo lo que sé de él me llega por vía escrita … sin embargo, no hay caso: no consigo verlo del todo como un escritor. Es más: muchas veces tengo la impresión de que esa identidad—la identidad "literaria" de Bellatin—no es otra cosa que un *trompe l'oeil*, una especie de alias.
>
> (Pauls 2005: np)

> It is hard for me to imagine Mario Bellatin as a writer. For a few years now I've only read him, everything I know about him has come to me through writing … but it's no use: I can't see him entirely as a writer. What is more, I often get the sense that this identity—Bellatin's "literary" identity—is a *trompe l'oeil*, a kind of alias.

Like the writers who were both present and absent at the *Congreso de Dobles*, Bellatin's authorial persona flits into and out of sight, sometimes asserting itself as an organizing principle, other times actively dismantling the interpretive apparatus erected around it. These operations, or literary games, find him shuttling between the acts of authoring a text and of authoring himself *as* a text ultimately subject to symbolic appropriation.

It makes sense, then, that the *Congreso de Dobles* forms part of a moment when Bellatin is adopting different literary personae in his writing—in notably Bellatinian ways. Two years before the conference in Paris, Bellatin published *Shiki Nagaoka: una nariz de ficción* (2001) [*Shiki Nagaoka: A Nose for Fiction* trans. David Shook 2012], which presents itself as the biography of a Japanese writer with a small but dedicated following and a very large nose. The whole thing, as we might expect, is a fabrication: Bellatin invented Shiki one day at a conference when asked, to his annoyance, to name a literary influence on his work. Further complicating the questions of lineage (intellectual and otherwise) and of legitimacy (the truth of a story and who gets to tell it) that attend the genre, the premise of this spurious biography is drawn from the 1916 short story "Hana" ["The Nose"] by Ryūnosuke Akutagawa: the story is about a monk known for his exceptionally large nose and is, in turn, based on a thirteenth-century tale. In other words, *Shiki Nagaoka* is the biography of a fictional Japanese writer based on the fiction of a real one, which was itself an adaptation. Moreover, both source texts appear as epigraphs to the novel and as appendices in the volume; Akutagawa's is described as being, perhaps, "an inspired account of our author's life" (Bellatin 2012: 17). Bellatin does like to play his games out in the open. Translation figures prominently in *Shiki Nagaoka*, as well. After learning the languages at the age of fifteen, Shiki Nagaoka "began to write his literary texts in English or French, to later convert them into his mother tongue, thereby achieving the effect that everything from his pen resembled a translation," because, far from subscribing to the notion of translation as loss, our protagonist argues that "only by means of reading translated texts does the real essence of the literary ... become evident" (2012: 13). Not only is the practice central to our protagonist's creative development, as Martín Gaspar has observed, it also acts as a buffer and strategy of denaturalization.[3]

Next came *Jacobo el mutante* (2002) [*Jacob the Mutant* trans. Jacob Steinberg 2015], for which Bellatin assumes the role of a literary

---

[3] Gaspar asserts that "Nagaoka is not a cosmopolitan writer; instead, he learns Western languages in order to *pass through them*, using them like shields" so as not to be claimed by one of the competing politico-aesthetic factions around him (2014: 130).

scholar who uncovered an unpublished novel by the Austrian writer Joseph Roth, identified in the Spanish text as *La frontera* (*The Border*, in Jacob Steinberg's English edition). Of this mysterious and distinctly mystical story about Jacob Pliniak, a former rabbi and the owner of a roadside tavern who is suddenly transformed into an elderly woman named Rosa Plinianson, "a complete translation has yet to surface, although fragments have shown up" (Bellatin 2015: 6). Entire sections of this novel are presented as these translated fragments attributed to an internationally recognized writer who did not, in fact, pen them. Further complicating this literary forgery, it turns out that (the real) Joseph Roth did in fact write a text called "Die Grenze" or "The Border," and that he was indeed associated with the German publishing houses Bellatin names in his novel.

The intermingling of fabrication and verifiable fact in both works is a recurring element of Bellatin's games, as is the presence of a supposedly subordinate text that engages and destabilizes the primary one.[4] Though Bellatin's use of the translator's footnote will be the primary focus of this chapter, his use of photography in *Shiki Nagaoka* and *Jacobo el mutante* (as in many other works) sheds light on the status and function of these annotations in *El jardín de la señora Murakami* (2000) [*Mrs. Murakami's Garden* trans. Heather Cleary 2020]. Alan Pauls has also noted the connection between text and image in Bellatin's work, describing it as "an unsettling aesthetic economy" in which "the story could be the epigraph, the footnote, the prologue or the epilogue of the image ... the written word reveals itself as insufficient and calls to the image; the image is never quite enough and longs for the written word" (Pauls 2005: np).

Though they do not serve a uniform purpose across the writer's oeuvre, photographs typically are not illustration of, but rather a

---

[4] Also key to Bellatin's production, and not insignificant in the context of the present study, is a sustained practice of re-publishing his work in Spanish, adding and subtracting images and text from each iteration. Two examples among many are his *Jacobo Reloaded* (Sexto Piso 2014) and multiple editions of *Perros héroes* [Hero dogs] that take divergent approaches to the relationship between image and text.

counterpoint to, the text alongside which they appear. They also hint at a narrative beyond the one presented: Bellatin often uses photography in a way that acknowledges its traditional documentary function while simultaneously undermining its status as such. In *Shiki Nagaoka*, for example, images are presented as "Photographic Documentation" (2012: 46), establishing the veracity of the (specious) author's biography. Though it goes without saying that the images are not what they claim to be, they are presented according to the conventions of biography: here the author's parents, there an early manuscript; here a few locations key to the author's life, there the elaborate tools used to wring oil from his exceptionally large nose. *Jacobo el mutante*, on the other hand, is punctuated with photographs in which diminutive spheres are scattered against the textured backdrop of a desert terrain, creating an enigmatic parallel narrative: the objects appear to be moving in space over time, but their meaning and relation to the story of Jacob Pliniak are left unexplained. Ximena Berecochea, who is responsible for the photographs that appear in both *Shiki Nagaoka* and *Jacobo el mutante*, wrote of her series *Desert*, comprised of images very similar to the ones that appear in *Jacobo el mutante*, that it, "deals with the referential character of the photographic image from the intentional generation of blind spots," blind spots that in turn afford the viewer a wide range of interpretive possibilities.[5]

Bellatin makes use of the translator's footnote in precisely this way in *El jardín de la señora Murakami*. Given his aversion to narratives that resolve neatly, to the sacrosanct figure of the Author, and to the notion of the text as a fixed, self-contained object, it is not surprising that Bellatin would be drawn to translation, yet while all three novels written during this period evoke translation as a major thematic or structural element, the one that engages the practice most deeply is the one that does not mention it by name. *El jardín de la señora Murakami* is a pseudotranslation complete with commentary and glosses on the

---

[5] http://www.ximenaberecochea.com/home#/desert (accessed October 28, 2019).

plot and on the Japanese (or Japanese-adjacent) terms that appear throughout. This conceit, as I will discuss below, allows Bellatin to usurp—and unravel from within—the discursive privilege of its imagined author in much the same way as the *Congreso de Dobles* did with its real ones. In fact, Bellatin describes the two projects as part of the same attempt "to get to the bottom of the relationship between the text and its author" (2006a: 110). In the pages that follow, I will explore Bellatin's mobilization of the paratextual space of the translator's footnote in *El jardín de la señora Murakami* to destabilize the idea of the author as privileged "owner" of either the text or its interpretation, and to challenge the status of the original as a cohesive object to which a stable interpretation can be attached. While the footnote—that marginal textual space in which the translator becomes visible—reveals the process that moves the body text from one place to another, it simultaneously complicates this transfer, threatening to trip it up.

I. On the (Foot-)Printed Page

Though it may appear innocuous—even, as Anthony Grafton has quipped, "apocalyptically trivial" (1994: 54)—the footnote has generated its share of polemics over the years. A repository for the excesses and shortcomings of the body text, the foot of the page is home not only to data and scholarly references, but also to declarations of intellectual affinity and enmity, corrections, anecdotes, and—in the case of the translator's note—particularly troublesome linguistic knots. Nonetheless, despite the fecundity of these textual latitudes, as Jacques Derrida points out in the address "This is Not an Oral Footnote," the footnote has historically been seen as subordinate to the text upon which it offers commentary:

> The status of a footnote implies a normalized, legalized, legitimized distribution of the space, a spacing that assigns hierarchical relationships … This relationship of authority inscribed in the topology

has a political dimension as well, indeed a theologico-political one ... the law of this hierarchy ... binds the author of the main text, the God of the footnoted text, to subordinates, slaves, or foreign annotators.

(1991: 193)

This theologico-political hierarchy, however, is not written in stone. Although the footnote is always "before the law" of the institutionally enforced hierarchy privileging the sacred word of the annotated text— or, rather, precisely because it is—the annotation has the potential to undermine that authority from the outset; as Derrida goes on to assert, "as soon as there is a law, *the* law—all deceptions, transgressions, and subversions are possible" (194).[6] In the end, the subordinate status of the footnote—also described as a "parasite" affixed to the annotated text (200)—is not as inevitable as it initially appears: certain practices of reading and writing may invert the relation between the two spaces. This central paradox is already evident in the title of Derrida's remarks: evoking Magritte's surrealist conceit, his intervention situates itself at the tenuous border between poiesis and commentary, that is, at the moment an object is reconstituted by the introduction of a gloss.

Setting aside for a moment the creative dimensions of the translator's intervention in the text, we see that the translator's footnote exists at the intersection of two contradictory mandates: the fidelity of "subordinates, slaves, and foreign annotators" and the autonomy of the commentator, who occupies a position of critical distance. In "N. de la T.: los pies del texto" (2008) [T.N.: the feet of the text], Liliana Feierstein suggests that the translator's footnote functions as a commentary just like the Talmudic *perush* do: at the same time they elucidate the text, they reveal its discourse to be subject to a chain of hermeneutic and

---

[6] In "For a Political Economy of Annotation," Laurent Mayali also argues that the struggle for discursive power is inscribed in the footnote itself. "In its original Latin meaning," he writes, "*auctor* does not designate the writer but rather the guarantor, that is, a person who attests or vouches for the truth of a statement or a situation ... this guaranteed reproduction of truth is embodied in the text, which in turn becomes a source of power. The annotation is thus a procedure of political appropriation of the power of the text" (1991: 185-6).

dialogic interventions. This commentary, which Feierstein describes as "constitutive, enriching, inescapable, infinite," transports and mobilizes the body text, "surrounding it and shaking from it the dust of centuries in its infinite interpretive possibilities" (2008: 18).[7] An unavoidable consequence of this exegesis is that—in the essential multiplicity it reveals—the footnote undermines the hermeneutic unity of the body text and, along with it, any claim to a single, privileged interpretation.

Feierstein understands the footnote as a subversive force that splinters "the homogeneity and transparency of the linear body of the text, forcing us to interrupt the monotonous rhythm of the monologue in a leap to the margin of the page, reminding us of the polyphony and multiplicity of meanings that textual dogma tried to conceal" (18). Beyond its function as a visual reminder of the translator's intervention—and of the gaps and misalignments inherent to any transfer between languages—the footnote also renders relative the discursive authority of the body text by presenting it alongside its commentary.[8] Although (or precisely because) these annotations illuminate "the complex interstices between languages," their presence is often challenged by conservative literary professionals who long for a text "without chaos, interruptions, or detours" (19).

Two short stories from different national and historical contexts in Latin America illustrate thematically (and visually) the footnote's ability to overturn discursive hierarchies and generate static in the primary narrative in a way that illuminates Bellatin's mobilization of the translator's note in *El jardín de la señora Murakami*.[9] The first of

---

[7] All translations of Feierstein's Spanish are my own, including the text of the epigraph.

[8] Though he acknowledges that the footnote has historically been used as a means of creating "a myth of scholarly authority," and even as he valorizes one form of marginal intervention over another, Grafton also recognizes that footnotes are "inevitably provisional; they invite criticism and revision" (1997: 59) and asserts that they serve as a counterpoint to the "intellectual dogmatism" of Descartes (1997: 66). Even within a scholarly context, then, the footnote performs a dialogic democratization of the text, belying the historian's claim to absolute discursive authority.

[9] For alternate readings of both short stories, see Rosemary Arrojo's *Fictional Translators* (2018).

these, Rodolfo Walsh's 1967 "Nota al pie" ["Footnote"], takes place in the wake of a suicide: León de Sanctis, a prolific but disillusioned translator, has taken his own life in the small quarters he rents, leaving behind an unfinished manuscript and a note addressed to his editor (and, it would appear, only friend), Otero. The text communicates just as much visually as it does through exposition: the space of the page is divided between the "narrative"—the action that occurs in the translator's room as Otero waits with León's landlady for the police inspector to arrive—and the "gloss" of a suicide note ostensibly left by the deceased. The thematic presentation of translation is complemented by the story's layout on the page, which is not only a visual representation of the subordinate position of the translator, but also forces the reader to move between the two texts, negotiating two parallel, and occasionally contradictory, accounts.

Within this pointedly hierarchical narrative structure, however, Walsh contests the traditional conception of the translator as a submissive, secondary producer of texts. Though he is presented as a solitary, impoverished, marginalized figure—adding a layer of irony to the fact that his name means "lion"—León is determined to create a space of agency for himself within his work. The footnote to the narrative asserts, in León's voice: "Nunca leí con anticipación el libro que traducía: así participaba en la tensión que se iba creando, asumía una parte del autor" (1967: 111) [I never read ahead in the book I was translating: that way, I participated in the tension that was building, I took on some part of the author]. At another point, he admits: "Resolvía cualquier dificultad omitiéndola. Un día extravié medio pliego de una novela de Asimov. ¿Sabe lo que hice? Lo inventé de pies a cabeza" (118) [I solved every problem by omission. One day I misplaced several pages of a novel by Asimov. Know what I did? I made it up from head to toe].

León's assertion of creative autonomy is represented on a structural level in the narrative, as well: unlike traditional footnotes, which form a network of data supplementary to the body text and joined to it by multiple glossed terms, the titular footnote turns out to be a parallel text, supplementary to the central narrative only insofar as it offers a different perspective on León's death. In the spatial representation of this discursive incursion, the translator's footnote—the suicide letter—occupies a mere two lines on the story's first page, but annexes more and more visual-discursive space as the ratio between "narrative" and "gloss" is gradually inverted. The final page features a single line of dialogue, which assigns ownership of the suicide note, lost in the italicized sea of the letter's content. What begins as a whispered apology becomes a roar that drowns out the body text—an operation in direct opposition to the elision to which León is subjected editorially, whether in the form of the abbreviation of his name to the nearly anonymous "L.D.S." or the removal of several dozen footnotes that had peppered his first translation.

Moacyr Scliar's 1995 short story "Notas ao pé da página" ["Footnotes"] takes a different approach to the power dynamics between author and translator, and by extension those between central and peripheral textual spaces. In contrast to the "relentless excision" (1967: 110) that Walsh's translator describes, Scliar presents a text that is *all* footnote: the original, which would typically occupy a central place on the printed page, has been excised completely from the document and it exists only through the references to it that appear in the footnotes. Most of the physical space of the page is left blank, and the only text to appear is the first-person response of a translator to a source text, supposedly the diary of the author with whom he works. Scliar's divergence from the cliché of the translator as a subjugated and shadowy figure is evident from the very start. Unlike Walsh's León, who—though cavalier in his treatment of the texts he translates and proud to a fault of his interventions—is portrayed as a recluse with one suit and a chronic case of sinusitis, Scliar's narrator is a swaggering aficionado, a translator of great renown invited to stay with the poet whose work he translates because this poet wanted to "estabelecer contatos com pessoas que lhe pareciam importantes— uma categoria na qual eu me enquadrava por minha reputação como tradutor" (1995: 372) [build relationships with people who seemed important to him—a category into which I fell because of my reputation as a translator]. The inversion of the translator's subservience is pronounced: the translator depicts the poet as waiting anxiously for his arrival and, later, begging on his knees—first that he not steal his lover and then, having failed in this, that at least he continue to translate his poetry. The story's final footnote describes the scene: "O autor também não fala da áspera discussão que tivemos ... Ofendeu-me tanto que, exasperado, anunciei-lhe que nunca mais traduziria um único verso dele. Nesse momento mudou por completo; praticamente arrojando-se a meus pés—era de uma submissão abjeta" (375) [The author *also fails to mention* the bitter argument we had, "the translator asserts." He made me so angry that I told him, furious, that I would never translate another line of his poetry. He changed his tune completely, practically *throwing himself at my feet*—he was deplorably submissive] (my italics).

Beyond inverting the hierarchy that would traditionally favor the original over its commentary, the image of the author occupying the space at the narrator's feet actually puts him *in the place* of the translator and inverts the parasitic relationship assumed to exist between author and translator, original and iteration. Similarly, with the opening negation of the passage just cited, Scliar reimagines the process of textual creation: not only is the "original" excised from the story, its invisible content is reconfigured—or generated for the first time, as in this case—by the translator, who adds in "missing" material. The fact that here the original is completely eclipsed by the voice of the translator points to a reality too often suppressed: that the translated text always reaches the reader through a process of refraction. It is always a retelling in another voice, despite pressures to conceal the process of mediation that brings the work into its new context. In fact, all five of the footnotes that comprise Scliar's story "clarify" a point in the absent text—as might be expected, given their assigned function as glosses—however, each and every one does so in the form of a refutation or through the insertion of material the author had intended to leave out. Scliar's text, then, presents the footnote as a space not of elaboration, but one of contestation, of negation. The translator asserts the power of his speech over that of the author, even to the extent that he *rewrites* the history being presented. Echoing the narrative's visual conceit—that is, the complete elision of the original and its replacement by commentary from the margins of the text—Scliar thus presents the footnote as a space from which not only glosses, elaborations, and corrections, but also *declarations* can be made.

Returning to Walsh's "Nota al pie," we see that its relationship to discursive authority is more complex than is immediately evident. Though the footnote that occupies the space allotted the translator at the bottom of the page in Walsh's story, and which expands so markedly over the course of the narrative, is credibly presented as the voice of the deceased translator, there is ample reason to believe that these words are not actually León's. Otero appears in León's quarters because he has been told that his employee left a suicide note addressed to him, but he does not open the letter when it is handed to him "porque quiere imaginar la versión que el muerto le daría si pudiera sentarse frente a él" (91) [because he *wants to imagine* the version that the dead man would give him if he could be sitting in front of him] (my italics). This is one of two times Otero is described as imagining León's words on the first page alone. In fact, the suicide note remains sealed and tucked away in Otero's pocket at the end of the story. The interpretation that the content of the letter is a product of the mind of its *recipient* is further supported by the way Walsh joins it to the body text: the word "lamento," which appears first as a noun and then as a first-person verb, acts as a hinge joining these two divergent textual spaces—both to one another, and to Otero's act of imagining, mentioned a second time just a few lines after the instance quoted above.

> [Otero] escucha la voz de la señora Berta que lo mira con sus ojos celestes y secos … murmurando que ya viene el comisario, y por qué no abre la carta. Pero no la abre aunque imagina su tono general de lúgubre disculpa, su primera frase de adiós y de lamento.*

> *Lamento dejar interrumpida la traducción que la Casa me encargó. Encontrará usted el original sobre la mesa, y las ciento treinta páginas ya traducidas. (91)

[Otero] hears Señora Berta, who is looking at him with her dry, pale blue eyes, muttering that the inspector is on his way, why not open the letter. But he doesn't, though he does imagine its general tone of gloomy apology, its opening phrase of farewell and regret.*

---

*I regret having left the translation commissioned by the Press unfinished. You will find the original on the table, along with the hundred and thirty pages already translated.

The parallel accounts that comprise the story, then, are joined by Otero's *imagining* what contents of the letter might be: first he chooses his imagined version of the letter over the letter itself as a means of protecting his memory of the deceased, then he chooses not to open the letter because he imagines that he already knows its contents. The repetition of this imagining, coupled with the use of the "lamento" as a rhetorical bridge between the two textual spaces, situates the suicide letter—and the subjectivity it is meant to project—in an unstable no-man's land between Otero's speech and León's. Though León, in many ways the archetypal translator, dutifully occupies the space allotted at the margins of the narrative (in the story, he is no more than a shrouded corpse), the nature of his presence there generates more questions than it answers. It asks, especially, the extent to which León's "final words" are really his own. In this sense, these stories posit the marginal space of the footnote not only as one in which to usurp discursive power, but rather as a space of hermeneutic instability that retroactively destabilizes the body text—a gesture that Mario Bellatin carries to the extreme in *El jardín de la señora Murakami*.

II. The Hermeneutic (Com-)Motion

In *The Art of Transition*, Francine Masiello suggests that recourse to the imaginary of the Far East in Latin American literature serves as a means of short-circuiting European cultural hegemony, allowing the writer to "dismantle the authority of the North/South map" and invite "a critique of hierarchical, modernist desire" (2001: 144) that reconfigures the cartography of cultural authority. Few contemporary writers can be said to engage the otherness of the Far East, and specifically that of Japan in a more sustained way than Mario Bellatin, in whose work geographic displacement is the condition of possibility of a broader process of "Brechtian *estrangement*" (Palaversich 2003: 28). It bears mention that Bellatin grew up in Peru, a country with significant cultural and demographic ties to Japan; nonetheless, the presence and manipulation of author signs such as Jun'ichirō Tanizaki, Yasunari Kawabata, Yukio Mishima, and Ryūnosuke Akutagawa—alongside his own inventions, like Shiki Nagaoka—are not grounded in familiarity, but rather suggest a key to understanding that is always just out of reach, perpetually deferring the consolidation of meaning.[10]

Consistent with this tendency, there are many references to Japanese literary tradition embedded in *El jardín de la señora Murakami*. Prominent among these is the work of Yasunari Kawabata: the novel's secondary title—*Oto no-Murakami monogatari*—echoes both Kawabata's *The Sound of the Mountain* (*Yama no Oto*) and the monogatari tradition—one of the most famous examples of which, the eleventh-century *Tale of Genji* (*Genji Monogatari*) is attributed to the noblewoman Murasaki Shikibu—who in turn provides Mr. Murakami's trusted servant with her name in Bellatin's novel. Kawabata also seems to have inspired the name of the novel's protagonist with his 1926 short story "The Dancing Girl of Izu," and his 1968 Nobel lecture—together with Tanizaki's *In Praise of Shadows*—likely

---

[10] For more on the cultural presence of Japan in Bellatin's life and work, and in Peru more broadly, see Rebecca Tsurumi's *The Closed Hand* (2012) and Ignacio López-Calvo's *The Affinity of the Eye: Writing Nikkei in Peru* (2013).

inspired many of the reflections on the tensions between tradition and modernity that appear in *El jardín de la señora Murakami*.[11]

Filtering his writing through the Western imaginary of Japanese literature has implications for Bellatin's project in both an aesthetic and a thematic sense. Stylistically, it allows Bellatin to further explore forms of narration that emerge from a place "of silence, of scarcity" (Bellatin 2006a: 109), which in turn denaturalize his writings and force the reader to consider their place of enunciation. The cultural and linguistic distance between Spanish and Japanese also allows Bellatin room to maneuver more freely in his games of authorial hide-and-seek, particularly through recourse to the mediating layers of translation as a means of probing the limits of textual unity and discursive authority. This is especially true of *El jardín de la señora Murakami*, which presents itself as a translation in everything from its secondary title, mentioned above, to the numerous footnotes that at once explicate and complicate the terms they gloss, and the "conventional" italicization of terms that actually appear in Spanish or are recognizable loan words (such as *futón* and *Formica*).

The foregrounding of the Japanese literary tradition within a Spanish-language novel has resonances on a thematic level, too. In *El jardín de la señora Murakami*, the negotiation of difference (in many cases, diametrical opposition) plays a fundamental role. At the center of the narrative is Izu, a young woman who dedicates herself to a career in art criticism and writes an article on the private collection of the wealthy, enigmatic Mr. Murakami. They marry not long thereafter, but the critical tone of Izu's article has major implications for both her domestic and professional life: her future husband stipulates that her family must disown her, her mentors turn their backs on her, and she is subjected to a series of spousal abandonments and humiliations that culminate in her removal from her husband's will and the destruction

---

[11] Martín Gaspar argues that the floating, "impersonal" tone of the body text of *El jardín de la señora Murakami* is inspired by *The Tale of Genji*, as well (2014: 181). My thanks to Sayuri Oyama for the illuminating conversation we had about Kawabata's work in November of 2019.

of her sanctuary, the garden attached to their house. As a young woman aspiring to professional success in a traditionally patriarchal society, Izu is forced to negotiate the cultural extremes of tradition and progress, of Eastern and Western aesthetics and practices, and—with a distinct metafictional inflection—of the real and the simulacrum, all of which appear in various ways throughout the novel.[12]

Evoking and physicalizing this leitmotif of shuttling between two worlds, the reader's eye shuttles constantly between the narrative and the bottom of the page, to the translator's footnotes inserted throughout. These notes, however, do more than relativize the discursive authority of the original: despite their tone of scholarly neutrality, most of the thirty-eight footnotes flout the conventions of the genre and present information that subtly but incontrovertibly undermines the text's internal logic. Many of these, like the photographs that accompany the biography of Shiki Nagaoka, are plausible at first glance but quickly give the reader a sense that something is … a bit off. For example, the note attached to the term *kimono* describes the article of clothing as a "traje tradicional confeccionado especialmente por mujeres" (Bellatin 2000: 9) [traditional garment typically made by women (Bellatin 2020: 7)] while the next note presents the *obi* as a belt, "cuyas medidas suelen tomarse de las figuras de las diosas en la religión shintoísta" (9) [the measurements of which are based on the figures of Shinto goddesses (7)]. Though understated when read in isolation, these examples pave the way for more audacious moves.

---

[12] Among these images of opposition is the game of three white stones against three black stones, seemingly derived from the ancient game of Go (which itself is enigmatically defined in the footnotes as a separate practice, making it even harder to identify the other game, which had such an impact on young Izu's life). Izu's extensive wardrobe, which consists of both modern (Western) clothes and traditional kimonos and their accoutrements—and which Bellatin describes in great detail—is another key example: as Bellatin explained to Emily Hind, "I was interested in clothes as a way to highlight the moment as a time of rupture, which relates back to the rupture in Peru and Latin America in the sixties" (Hind 2002: 23).

Some of the footnotes that appear in the novel, like the description of *somobono*, an apocryphal delicacy favored by Mr. Murakami, require the reader to do a bit of research to uncover the feint. Others unravel themselves within the space of just a few lines. Such is the case with the footnote that glosses the familiar term "haiku," which reads simply: "Forma poética que demuestra la inutilidad de los grandes tratados filosóficos, según palabras del sabio Surinami Mayoki (1113–1128)" (64) [A poetic form that demonstrates the uselessness of the great philosophical treatises, according to the sage Surinami Mayoki (1113–1128) (57)]. Not only does this note deviate from the standard definitions of haiku, it renders the term more opaque, rather than clearer, through its intervention. Asserting the haiku's capacity to unmask the uselessness of the "great philosophical treatises," the note cites a sage who appears to have lived to be a mere fifteen years old. This combination of explicit and veiled misdirection casts doubt on the entire hermeneutic system that the glosses sustain. Through this anti-explicatory stance, the footnote sheds its subaltern administrative function and asserts itself as a parallel, independent, enigmatic text that—it could easily be argued—demands its own annotative apparatus.

> se de pie en uno de los senderos acuáticos.
>   La muerte del marido fue un trance penoso. Pasó los últimos días en un delirio constante en el cual pidió a gritos la presencia nada menos que de Etsuko, la antigua *saikokú*[1] de su mujer. El esposo quería ver nuevamente sus pechos. Al principio la señora Murakami pretendió no entender aquellos reclamos. Hacía oídos sordos a sus palabras y buscó siempre mantener una actitud serena al lado de la cama del moribundo. Únicamente Shikibu advirtió el pálido rubor de sus mejillas, que aparecía sobre todo cuando el marido hablaba de Etsuko delante del médico.
>
> [1] Véase nota 5.

Figure 3.1 Image of page 8 of *El jardín de la señora Murakami*.

This manipulation and usurpation of discursive authority from the margins of the page is consciously foregrounded in the novel. In fact, Bellatin announces it with the very first footnote. This note is attached to the term *saikokú*, which appears twice early in the narrative: first, in the description of Mr. Murakami's death—which was, as Bellatin writes, a terrible ordeal. "He spent his final days in a constant state of delirium, calling for none other than Etsuko, his wife's former *saikokú*.¹" Flouting convention, the gloss attached to the term reads, simply, "See note 5" (6), deferring the expected definition.

It is only when we get to the next section of the narrative that we are offered any sort of explanation of what the term might mean. The sentence in the body text to which the much-anticipated fifth footnote is attached asserts that Izu appeared one morning at her future husband's door "acompañada por Etsuko, su fiel sirvienta.⁵" [accompanied by Etsuko, her faithful servant.⁵] The note, in its entirety, reads:

> 5. En realidad, una *saikokú*, tal como se entendía ese oficio en el periodo imperial. Sus funciones estaban a medio camino entre sirvienta, ama de llaves, doncella o dama de compañía. Las *saikokús* desempañaban todas estas funciones y al mismo tiempo ninguna.
>
> (14)

> 5. In reality, a *saikokú*, as the role was understood in imperial times: something between servant, housekeeper, escort, and chaperone. *Saikokús* performed all these functions and, at the same time, none.
>
> (11)

Rather than elucidating the term to which it is attached—servant—the footnote presents the content withheld before, despite the fact that the definition no longer lines up with its referent. In fact, the information is presented as a correction or refutation of the body text: Etsuko is not, as the author of the primary text claims, a servant, but is instead a member of a particular class of domestic help. Similarly, note 34 also refers to the term *saikokú*, but directs the reader back to note four, which is about *kabuki* theater rather than the unique form of domestic employment treated in note five. This gesture of deferral is repeated in several other footnotes, creating a web of mis- or redirection that renders nearly impossible any effort to move through the text in a linear way.

Other footnotes go a step beyond dashing expository expectations to present themselves as aporias: interventions that hinder, rather than facilitate, cross-cultural understanding. In a description of yet another fake food item (the prevalence of these in the novel is a neat metaphor for the consumption of simulacra), Bellatin describes Izu's view through the ground floor windows of a modern building. "Había una gran barra con la gente comiendo de pie. En las vitrinas que daban a la calle se exhibían los *sushi*[26], *ramen*[27], y *mategeshin*[28] de cera" (57) [There was a long counter inside where people ate standing up. In the windows facing the street were plates of *sushi*,[26] *ramen*,[27] and *mategeshin*[28] made of wax (50)]. The footnotes that accompany these terms appear as follows:

The "translator" intervenes here solely to generate silence: first, in the form of a dismissive comment ("Typical dishes whose description would

> donde las hojas de ... ...
> congelarse.
> Cuando al fin llegó a casa del señor Murakami, Izu pareció arrepentirse de haber emprendido aquella travesía matinal. Durante la caminata había ido aminorando la importancia de su visita. Cuando advirtió que a pesar de las condiciones atmosféricas una anciana conducía una bicicle-
>
> [26] Platillos típicos cuya descripción no aportaría nada sustancial al relato.
> [27]
> [28]
>
> 57

Figure 3.2 Image of page 57 of *El jardín de la señora Murakami*.

add nothing substantial to the story"), then as the literal withholding of the expected gloss. Unlike many translational silences, this one does not arise from the limitations of language but is instead a marker of the translator's refusal to perform the function assigned to him. By choosing not to render intelligible the selected terms—either through translation or through a gloss at the foot of the page—the translator establishes his autonomy relative to the original text and asserts that it is for him to decide which of the culturally specific terms merits explication, based on his interpretation of the narrative and his assessment of its most relevant elements. In some ways, this gesture is reminiscent of Scliar's "Footnotes," which presents a translator relegated to the margins of the page but who nonetheless exerts a constitutive force on the "original." There is a key difference, however: in Scliar's story, the blank space where the body text should be is a marker of what Rosemary Arrojo has described as a "will to power" (2018: 79), a desire to control not only the writing, but also the interpretation of the work. The translator in "Notas ao pé da página" suppresses completely the author's voice, and the white of the page is the scar left by his excision from the narrative. In *El jardín de la señora Murakami*, the blank space on the page—this time in the footnotes—likewise signals an assertion of power on the part of the translator, but here it represents a rift: it disrupts the flow of the narrative to remind the reader of the distance between languages that translation may sometimes appear to overcome, but never without the active intervention of a translator who arrives to the text with a complete set of subjective predispositions already in place. As a result, the text is not a stable object able to render a consolidated meaning but will always be a site of competition among these different layers of interference.

The destabilizing effect produced by Bellatin's footnotes, then, does not only "increase the reader's disorientation through false or unnecessary definitions," as Emily Hind has suggested (2002: 24). Insisting on the work's status as a translation, the footnotes of *El jardín de la señora Murakami* render the text a palimpsest, the meaning of which is consolidated and dissipates as the trace of its other potential versions moves in and out of focus, generating a form of hermeneutic interference or static. It is a process that directly engages the notion that the function of this textual space is limited to ensuring that the "theological" meaning of the body text be transmitted. Ultimately, the feet of this text carry it further and further from territories in which any singular, authoritative, interpretation might be imposed.

El jardín de la señora Murakami is not Bellatin's first, or only, use of the footnote as a space for literary games. In 2008, Bellatin composed a piece called "El abrazo del abismo" ["The Embrace of the Abyss"] for *ADN*, the cultural supplement of the Argentine newspaper *La Nación*. The text was about none other than the Japanese writer Yasunari Kawabata. After opening with the question of what would happen if the "sentimental threads" that entwine and define a literary tradition were to disappear—an effect that could plausibly describe his own writing— Bellatin performs what appears to be a rote critical gesture, a reference to the words of another critic about his subject.

> Para algunos críticos contemporáneos—cito el caso de Alan Pauls— se les hace difícil reconocer a Yasunari Kawabata como a un escritor. Alan Pauls afirma que desde hace algunos años no hace más que leerlo y aquello que sabe de él le llega por escrito. Y, sin embargo, no hay caso, no consigue verlo del todo como a un escritor. Su identidad—la identidad literaria Kawabata ... no es otra cosa que un *trompe l'oeil*, una especie de alias.
>
> (2008: np)

> Some contemporary critics—here I cite the case of Alan Pauls—find it hard to imagine Yasunari Kawabata as a writer. Alan Pauls asserts that for a few years now he's only read him, that everything he knows about him comes to him through writing. Still, it's no use: he can't see him entirely as a writer. His identity—the literary identity Kawabata ... is a *trompe l'oeil*, a kind of alias.

If this description sounds familiar, it's because these are the words Alan Pauls used to describe Bellatin three years earlier. This appropriation of Pauls's assessment makes his line about literary identity being a kind of alias all the more pointed. As it turns out, the entire article is composed of snippets written not about Kawabata, but about Bellatin, and reformulated for the purpose. As a complement to his invention of Shiki Nagaoka, here Bellatin uses an existing writer as a vehicle to dismantle the author sign from within.

One would have to be a diligent student of Bellatin's textual universe to pick up on this sleight of hand solely from what appears in the *ADN* article. According to its author, however, the piece and the game behind it were not meant to be obscure: a crucial element was missing from its original publication, in the form of a footnote that reveals the appropriative processes behind the piece. This footnote—or, rather, a message describing the phantom footnote—was published the following day on the blog of the Argentine writer and critic Daniel Link, along with the original text of the *ADN* article. In this complementary (as opposed to supplementary) intervention, Bellatin explains that the article was composed by assembling existing texts, written not about Kawabata, but about … him. "Dear L," he writes,

> te quería informar que ayer en *ADN* salió una nota mía sobre kawabata … envié la nota con un pie de página donde decía que había sido hecha con la técnica de copypaste (copyright 2008), pie que no apareció lamentablemente … para responderme una serie de preguntas hice ese texto juntando una serie de fragmentos que distintos críticos han hecho sobre mis libros … cambié la palabra bellatin y le puse kawabata, cambié el nombre de algunas obras y yastá … un artículo estupendo sobre kawabata, impecable en su verosimilitud y certeza.
>
> (Link 2008: np)

> i wanted to let you know that a note i'd written about kawabata came out in *ADN* yesterday … i'd sent a footnote along with it that said i'd made it using my copypaste technique (*copyright* 2008), a footnote that unfortunately appears nowhere … in response to a series of questions, i made this text by gathering a series of fragments that different critics have written about my books … i changed the word bellatin for kawabata, changed the names of a few texts and there you go … a fantastic article about kawabata, flawless in its verisimilitude and conviction.

Here again we see Bellatin's insistence on the transitive quality of authorial style and his devaluation of authorial aura, as exemplified by the lowercase letter at the beginning of proper nouns and the use of "word" instead of "name" in reference to the two writers (the texts, meanwhile, do get "names"). Beyond this, and of particular interest in the present context, we see a simultaneous writing and unraveling at work from the paratext. Whether Bellatin actually intended to publish the footnote as part of his piece in *La Nación*, or whether he had always conceived of it as a kind of spectral gloss, the essence of the gesture is the same: it is the mobilization of the space at the margin, not to elucidate or expand upon the body text, but rather to undermine its status as a cohesive whole framed by a single authorial perspective.

III. A Re-writer on the Edge

The last of the enigmatic footnotes that punctuate the narrative of *El jardín de la señora Murakami* serves as a hinge between the body text and the twenty-four notes that comprise the appendix, and demonstrates the extent to which this novel functions as the vehicle of its own unmaking. In the final passage of the narrative, the widow Murakami imagines that she sees, in the rubble of her garden as it is being dismantled, a small house at the base of a mountain. From within, she hears her father calling to her in a language that "le resulta imposible entender" (Bellatin 2000: 103) [she finds impossible to understand (Bellatin 2020: 94)]. The word she registers without understanding, the final word of the main narrative, is *otsomuru*—according to the footnote, a term that "se refiere a un final que es en realidad un comienzo. El poeta Bansho (1644–1694) la utilizaba en los poemas que no tenía previsto publicar" (103) [refers to an ending that is, in fact, a beginning. The poet Bansho (1644–1694) used it in the poems he did not plan to publish (94)]. Again, the footnote opens up an aporia within the narrative: first and foremost, by suggesting that a key term in the text is unintelligible to its protagonist and, second, that the term is drawn from an invisible body of work, in the Menardian sense. Moreover, the definition this final footnote offers of the novel's final word suggests that the end of the narrative is itself a beginning. A beginning, in that the accumulation of footnotes, culminating in the gloss of the term *otsomuru*, sends the reader back to the beginning of the novel to decode the entire thing again. Literally speaking, of course, the final note also marks the end of the principal narrative and the beginning of the appendix, which even more forcefully sends readers back to the starting block by withdrawing from them those elements of the plot upon which their interpretations had depended.

Although it is presented as a parallel discourse—in that the footnotes make no reference to the addenda, nor vice versa—these two peripheral textual spaces in which the translator asserts his visibility build on one another to chip away at the coherence of the central narrative. While the footnotes engage specific moments in the text and generally focus on specific terms, the addenda comment on the story as a whole, making corrections and adding information that would typically fall outside the translator's sphere of knowledge. The first addendum, for example, reads "1. Si bien no se explicita, la señora Murakami mantiene una extraña relación con el ensayo *Elogio de la sombra* de Tanizaki Yunichiro. Resulta imposible definir la naturaleza de tal interés." (105) [Though this is never stated explicitly, Mrs. Murakami has a strange relationship with Junichiro Tanizaki's essay *In Praise of Shadows*. The nature of her interest in the text is impossible to define (95)]. Not only does the comment demonstrate an extra-textual familiarity with the personal habits of the book's characters, the translator-as-commentator also sets the limits of how far this field of vision can be expanded. Several of the addenda fill in "missing" details—like the provenance and quality of the futons used by Izu's family, or the similarity of the hairstyle she wears to her husband's funeral to the one worn by the aunt of her first fiancé on the day he died of rabies (96)—while others flash forward to provide updates on what happens to several secondary characters later in life. In these addenda, as in the footnotes to the text, Bellatin reconfigures the relationship between the original and its version(s). Through textual interventions situated at the novel's margins and tied to its status as a translation, *El jardín de la señora Murakami* opens up rifts in the "original" work upon which it is supposedly dependent; in the addenda it often does so by citing points at which the narrative fails to convey aspects of the fictional world it represents that fall outside the scope of the story and then filling in those gaps. This is the case in the fifth addendum, which laments the absence of detail surrounding Mr. Murakami's domestic life during his illness ("5. Es imposible comprender por qué se ha omitido la narración del regreso del señor Murakami a la casa conyugal cuando supo que moriría de cáncer de próstata. Durante todo el tiempo que duró su enfermedad, Izu Murakami tuvo que cuidarlo como cualquier esposa diligente" [106] [The omission of Mr. Murakami's return home after learning he would die of prostate cancer is beyond comprehension. Izu Murakami cared for him throughout his illness, as any good wife would] [96]), and the twelfth, which informs us that Matsuei Kenzo and Aori Mizoguchi, two men "who were very important in Izu Murakami's life" were thought to be living together on the West Coast of the United States, and (in addendum sixteen) that nothing ever came of the art history textbook Kenzo was writing throughout the course of the novel (98). Other addenda take yet another step back from the text to offer editorial critiques on its composition, asserting that "7. En algún momento de la narración habría sido conveniente volver a referirse a la Cacería de Orugas, y tal vez explicar con detalle el absurdo de semejante actividad." (106) [It would have been a good idea to mention the Caterpillar Hunt at another point in the narrative, and perhaps to describe in greater detail how absurd the activity is (96)], or asking why it was never made clear whether or not Mr. Murakami knew how to drive (96).

These gestures of subterfuge come to a head in a note that refers to the culmination of Izu's domestic infelicity and the beginning of her financial ruin. Here, beyond the end of the story that is also a beginning, the "translator" forces the reader to reimagine the novel anew, asserting in the eighteenth addendum that:

> 18. Resulta difícil entender la actitud final del señor Murakami pidiendo a gritos volver a ver los pálidos pechos de Etsuko. Podría atribuirse a los efectos de los medicamentos y la agonía. Sin embargo, se cuenta con los elementos necesarios para incluso llegar a pensar que fueron amantes. Si eso es cierto, nunca se conocerán las verdaderas razones que motivaron a los protagonistas.
>
> (108)

> 18. It is hard to understand why Mr. Murakami demanded, at the end of his life, to see Etsuko's pale breasts again. The incident could perhaps be attributed to the medications he was taking, and the pain. Nonetheless, it contains all the elements required to imagine that the two might even have been lovers. If this is the case, the true motivations of the story's protagonists will never be known.
>
> (98–9)

These divergent explanations of Mr. Murakami's final request would be destabilizing or at least confusing in any context; here, however, they represent a direct attack on the comprehensibility of the text as a whole. Presenting an alternative hypothesis only to immediately reject it, Bellatin offers a logical conclusion (that Mr. Murakami and Etsuko were lovers) as the condition of the *im*possibility of interpreting the entire work: in other words, if this—very possible—thing is true, the motivations of our protagonists will never be known.

It is no coincidence that so many of these addenda mobilize the language of incomprehension, or that the complementary marginal space of the footnotes so often serves to obscure the meaning of the body text. As would be the case years later in the phantom footnote to his Kawabata article, it is ultimately incomprehension that Bellatin is driving at. Occupying the margin of his own text in the guise of the translator, he presents not a linear and authoritative narrative, but rather the chaotic sum of its "infinite interpretive possibilities" (Feierstein 2008: 18).[13]

But what is at stake in this resistance to intelligibility, and why are the translator's "parasitic" (Derrida 1991: 200) paratexts such a fertile space for these very serious games? Another translation may be in order. Michel Serres, in his classic study *Le Parasite*, serves up a useful complement to the familiar biological model of an organism that "feeds" (from sitos, or food) "next to" (para) another—eating at the table, or feeding upon the body, of the other. Riffing on the fact that, in French, the term "parasite" also refers to the static produced within an electronic signal, Serres offers a reading of the rats' feast from Bousault's *Fables d'Esope*, that lists a series of parasitic relationships, from the "tax farmer" who feeds off profits from his privileged position under the law—a bracing inversion of economic parasitism in the contemporary capitalist imaginary—to the country rat, who in turn feeds with his kin on the tax farmer's Persian rug. Suddenly, the scene is transformed: a burst of interference disturbs the rats' meal and they scurry off. "It was only a noise," writes Serres in Lawrence Schehr's nimble translation, "but it was also a message, a bit of information producing panic: an interruption, a corruption, a rupture of information. Was the noise really a message? Wasn't it, rather, static, a parasite? A parasite who has the last word, who produces disorder and who *generates a different order*" (2007: 3, my italics).

It may be that benefits only flow in one direction in the company of parasites, but this does not mean they bring nothing to the table. In this "bit of information" that erupts in the form of noise or static, the parasite generates a disturbance that reconfigures that which it disturbs. The disturbance created by Bellatin's footnotes and other translational paratexts, then, goes beyond simply inverting (and in so doing,

---

[13] In *Paratexts*, Gerard Genette similarly imagines "a more emancipated regime in which the note would no longer come under the heading of this documentary type of discourse, but would ... pursue some momentary fork in the narrative" (1977: 335–6). "To do this," he continues, now citing Paul Valéry, "would be to substitute for the illusion of a unique scheme which imitates reality that of the possible-at-each-moment" (336).

reproducing or reinforcing) the hierarchical relationship between the text and its commentary. In the context of debates surrounding the definition and dynamics of World Literature that reemerged with a late-capitalist spin around the time *El jardín de la señora Murakami* was published, Bellatin's footnotes challenge the very idea of a text as something that can be comprehended—and subsequently apprehended, neatly packaged, and transferred between parties like a good. Among other things, these paratexts are the static that produces disorder in the (illusion of) smooth interlinguistic, intercultural transfer upon which the prophets and profits of globalization depend. Of all the personae Bellatin adopted during this period in the early 2000s—pseudo-biographer, pseudo-literary historian, or handler of a band of pseudo-authors—it is the role of pseudo-translator that allows him to push the novel furthest from the strictures of ownership and dominion.

IV. Playing Along

The *mise en scène* of literary forgery is prominent throughout Bellatin's work. Several of his best-known texts play with the notion of the false translation, or even that of the false original. In a real-life performance of the literary production of one of his own characters—Shiki Nagaoka, who writes his texts "in English or French to later convert them into his mother tongue" so that "everything from his pen resembled a translation" (2012: 13)—Bellatin claims to have signed a contract with the French publishing house Gallimard to the effect that, rather than selling them the rights to a work already published in Spanish, he would send them an unpublished work to translate. The translator was to destroy the original after rendering it in French and, were the text ever to make it into the Latin American market, it would do so only as a translation from the Gallimard edition (Rohter 2009: np). He recently repeated the gesture (with variations) in a piece I requested for the *Buenos Aires Review*: the "prophetic translation" of a story titled

"Writing Lessons for the Blind and Deaf."[14] In the email correspondence that accompanies the story on the website, Bellatin and his long-time translator and collaborator David Shook discuss, in the future tense, the finer points of the text that Bellatin would—in theory, at some point—write.

Shook: Te adjunto las primeras 800 palabras, más o menos, de mi traducción de *Lecciones de Escritura para Personas Ciegas y Sordas*. ¿Cuando escribirás la obra, querrás decir con el título que los estudiantes son ciegos y sordos, al estilo Helen Keller, o que algunos son ciegos y otros son sordos?

Bellatin: Unos sordos, otros ciegos, pero quien cuenta el relato es sorda y ciega con un aparato por el cual logra oír algo que le transmite por medio de la computadora a un aparato braille electrónico a su hermano que sí es ciego y sordo de veras ....

Shook: Here are the first 800 words, more or less, of my translation of *Writing Lessons for the Blind and Deaf*. When you write the piece, will the title mean that the students are blind and deaf, like Helen Keller, or that some are blind and others deaf?

Bellatin: Some are deaf and others are blind, but the narrator is deaf and blind and uses a machine to be able to hear a few things, which he then transmits to his brother, who really is blind and deaf ...

(Bellatin 2015b: np)

In both these instances involving phantom originals, Bellatin situates himself as an author-sign that shapes the meaning of each text despite playing a dubious role in its creation.

What to do, then, when translating a writer so resistant to intellectual property and to what is generally understood as propriety? To what extent do Bellatin's transgressive interventions both on and off the page form part of the work to be translated? Is it enough to translate into English the text as it appears in Spanish, or does the work demand other

---

[14] The piece can be accessed in English at: http://www.buenosairesreview.org/2015/05/writing-lessons/

processes that hint at Bellatin's broader project, providing the kind of framework for reading that someone with access to his writing (and the extensive reflections written about it) in Spanish might have? And if so, what form could that intervention take?

Bellatin's translators into English seem to agree: his textual games leave plenty of room for us to play, too; indeed, they seem to demand that we do. The triptych of pseudobiography, literary scholarship, and translation—*Shiki Nagaoka*, *Jacobo el mutante*, and *El jardín de la señora Murakami*—was translated by three different individuals who each chose to extend Bellatin's gesture as we rewrote the work for an English-language readership. Jacob Steinberg, translator of *Jacobo el mutante*, echoes the mysticism of the original in a translator's note that instead of reflecting on the linguistic challenges of the text, describes the translator's own experience with the transmigration of souls. Steinberg ultimately claims that he understands Roth's (Bellatin's) narrative because he is, in fact, the reincarnation of his great-grandmother, Rose Eigen. Then, employing a very Bellatinian structure of vignettes, he goes on to trace the series of mutations that led to his discovery.

David Shook takes a more literary-critical tack in his translator's preface to *Shiki Nagaoka*, stating that he hopes "to redress his underacknowledgement as a major influence on contemporary world literature" (2012: np) and goes on to situate Bellatin's apocryphal biography within an invented literary history that ranges from a scholarly monograph written about the fake author by the real Mexican writer Pablo Soler Frost, to a special 1953 issue of *Life* magazine dedicated to Nagaoka's masterpiece that was promptly pulped in 1954 "when it was seized by customs officials and the New Jersey Port Authority on charges of obscenity" (np). Tapping into one of the recurring preoccupations of Bellatin's work, Shook attributes the dearth of translations into English of Nagaoka's work in the half century that followed this first attempt to the caprices of his estate, run by "a vain and shortsighted podiatrist" who refuses to release the rights to the work "on principle" (np). Once again, the treatment of creative works as private property keeps them from circulating as freely as they should; in fact, the claim to intellectual property is here posited as a first step on the way to erasure.

When thinking about how I wanted to approach my contribution to the English incarnation of *Mrs. Murakami's Garden*, a few things immediately became clear. A traditional translator's note wouldn't work: so much was happening beyond the level of the word that close readings seemed to miss much of the point, and explaining the game would be like offering a word-for-word translation of the novel: faithful on the micro level, but not at all to its spirit. I couldn't add my own footnotes, either, as those would have diluted the effect of Bellatin's.

I decided to focus on the original's embedded literary references, the questionable legitimacy of the text, and its central gestures of appropriation and play. I wrote an impassioned defense of the novel as a "true" translation, knowing full well that it was not. In order to bring the game further into the open, as Bellatin likes to do, my translator's note makes sustained references to "Pierre Menard, Author of the Quixote," Borges's seminal jaunt into questions of authorship, authority, and the mutability of the text. There's even a vilified French academic (initials H. B., in honor of Madame Henri Bachelier, egregious misrepresenter of Menard's work), who penned "a misguided scholarly article titled 'La Muse apocryphe: Tradition et trahison dans l'œuvre de Mario Bellatin,' in which [he] engages in a labyrinthine and utterly baseless discussion of the novel as a 'false' translation" (102). To refute this outrageous (entirely valid) claim, I offer a long list of (mostly) real and very *visible* works by the Mexican-Peruvian writer that blends the plausible and the absurd, including:

e) The lost original of a translation titled "Writing Lessons for the Blind and Deaf";
f) The definitive study of an undiscovered text by Joseph Roth;
g) A scholarly article on the history of the haiku, written as a haiku;
h) A collection of vignettes in which Bellatin asserts, then refutes, the validity of nostalgia (103–4)

Just as Borges does in "Pierre Menard," I read two identical passages from the "original" and Bellatin's translation—both of which are presented in English—that reveals how profoundly innovative the (absent) Spanish version is; I also employ Bellatin's patented "copypaste" technique, presenting remarks he made about other works (including his own) and snippets of a talk given at Stanford by David Shook as if they were Bellatin's reflections on the novel in question. Finally, and with all due respect, I make a few minor corrections to his otherwise exemplary translation and its annotations.

4

Writing off the Map

Somewhere between sacrifice and playfulness ... obedience and rebellion, assimilation and expression—there, in this apparently empty space, its temple and its clandestinity, is where the anthropophagous ritual of Latin American discourse is constructed.

— Silviano Santiago, *The Space In-Between*

Like Mario Bellatin's *El jardín de la señora Murakami*, Valeria Luiselli's *Los ingrávidos* (2011) [*Faces in the Crowd* trans. Christina MacSweeney 2014], centers on a false translation—though in this case it might be more appropriate to call it an act of interlinguistic ghost-writing. The novel consists of vignettes narrated by two individuals who claim to have died countless times; many of these vignettes involve the trace of the other appearing in each of their lives. In one storyline, a young mother in Mexico City tries desperately to carve out a space for her writing amid the responsibilities of raising two small children and the invasive and controlling gaze of a husband who reads what she writes after she falls asleep. The story she is trying to tell, which becomes the second of the novel's narrative worlds, is that of her previous life in New York City, when she worked as something like a scout and translator for an independent publisher in search of the next Bolaño. She discovers that the Mexican poet Gilberto Owen lived in Harlem from 1928 to 1930 and becomes increasingly immersed in his work and life. Unable to find an angle that her employer would find compelling enough to publish Owen in the US market, she decides to forge papers (which she presents in her English "translation") that link him to the objectivist poet Louis Zukovsky and Federico García Lorca, who was in Harlem studying at Columbia University and writing *Poeta en Nueva York* at the same time.[1] In so doing, she not only situates a reinvented Owen on the threshold of world literature, she also engenders a new Zukofsky: one who took an interest in a little-known Sinaloan poet while working on his masterpiece. Meanwhile, Owen narrates his experience—which alternatingly overlaps with, contradicts, or expands upon the young woman's research—in a parallel series of vignettes as the idea for a book of his own begins to take shape in his mind: a novel about a young woman he sees from time to time in the subway, whose features and actions match those of the narrator of the other storyline.

The fact that it is sometimes difficult to tell in which voice a given vignette is written is central to the (translational) logic of *Los ingrávidos*, and is tied to one of its key spaces: the New York City subway. María Pape has insightfully observed that the subway informs the organization of the novel in structural terms, insofar as the reader "pops out" at different fragments along the way—while the connections between them, the routes traveled, remain opaque (2015: 174). The reader is in constant movement, dropped into one perspective after another as both directionality and distance seem to lose footing. For all the characters in the novel, the subway is a privileged space of encounter. It is where the young woman meets Moby—an occasional lover and fellow forger of literary works—and where her friend Dakota occasionally busks; it also ties Owen to New York City through the coincidental fact that both came into being in 1904.[2] It is also where the "primera y última aparición pública de los Ojetivicios"

---

[1] On this point, Luiselli's novel resonates with Mariano Siskind's *Historia del Abasto* (2007), in which a young man moves to New York City and gets a job interviewing important cultural figures for a Buenos Aires newspaper; he meets his deadlines by translating interviews that he hears on NPR and sending them back as if he'd conducted them. Underscoring the character's complex relationship to the space(s) he occupies, and the collapse and simultaneous reassertion of the distance between these—a quality central to Luiselli's novel—Siskind titled the final sub-chapters of his novel "There (Here)" and "Here (There)."

[2] Luiselli (2014: 36). The note that appears on page 43 of the Spanish edition does not specify that it was also the year of Owen's birth, highlighting one of several adjustments made to the text for an anglophone readership.

(Luiselli 2011: 114) [first and last appearance of the Ohetivices (Luiselli 2014: 113)]—the name adopted by the Spanish-speakers in Zukovsky's fictional circle, tongues planted firmly in cheek—is staged. The performance is a remarkable piece of experimental translation: taking as their point of departure a passage from Zukovsky's epic poem, which they previously had him recite to them without informing him of their plans, in a "pasillo bien amplio del ferrocaril subterráneo" (2011: 114) [nice wide passage in the subway (2014: 113)] Owen and Lorca perform the work as simultaneous translations based predominantly on the phonetic aspect of the lines. This game of telephone is played somewhat differently in the Spanish and English editions of the novel, though in both cases Zukovsky's "original" is omitted—it, too, is a ghost haunting the text. In *Los ingrávidos*, one column offers a phonetic English intralinguistic "translation" ("These, itching and saying, 'behoover us'") accompanied by a rendition of those lines in Spanish ("Aquí le pica y dice, 'hoovereanos'"). In *Faces in the Crowd*, both Owen's and Lorca's interventions appear in English and could be described as sequential rounds in a game of telephone (Owen: "This, itching, is saying, 'behoover us,'" and Lorca: "In this kitchen insane: 'Hoover us'"), inviting a reflection on the unexpected possibilities of what is typically considered translation.[3]

The formulation of the subway as a zone of contact or translational space is not limited, however, to these anecdotes. The subway is, first and foremost, the site of the novel's foundational myth (and the source of its title in English): the moment when Ezra Pound catches sight of a friend who had been killed in the war months earlier and, shaken to his core, writes "In a Station of the Metro" with his body propped up against a column on the subway platform. This story is told once by the young woman, recounting the version told to her by her employer, and once by Owen, who believes (while disbelieving)

---

[3] Zukovsky's verse is, originally, "These, each in itself, is saying, 'behoove us,/Disprove us least as things of love appearing/In a wish gearing to light's infinite locus,/Balm or jewelweed is according to focus" (qtd. Miller 2009: 141). All quotations from this scene appear on page 114 of *Los ingrávidos* and 113 of *Faces in the Crowd*.

that he saw Pound on that platform in his moment of communion with the dead.[4] In a similar way, Owen is able to glimpse the young woman, and vice versa. On the day of his and Lorca's performance on the subway platform, he sees her walk past in her red coat, carrying the chair that, in the other storyline, the young woman admits to stealing from her place of employment; on another occasion, their trains run parallel for a moment and he is able to get a better look at her. She is reading his collected works, though he doesn't realize this. The subway, displacement made manifest, becomes a space in which time is reshaped.[5]

One of the notes that the young woman compiles about Owen (and the one that offers itself up as a starting point for the book she is trying to write about him) is a message he wrote to the Mexican theater director and filmmaker Celestino Gorostiza, which reads: "New York se le empieza a ver desde el *subway*. Acaba allí la perspectiva plana, horizontal. Empieza un paisaje de bulto ahí, con la doble profundidad, o eso que llaman cuarta dimensión, del tiempo" (Luiselli 2011: 44) [New York has to be seen from the viewpoint of the subway. The flat horizontal perspective vanishes in there. A bulky landscape begins, with the double depth, or what they call the fourth dimension, of time (Luiselli 2014: 37)]. Again, juxtaposition among the vignettes does heavy lifting in the construction of meaning in this novel: this note appears immediately after the young woman claims to have made eye contact with Owen on the subway, reinforcing that assertion. As a

---

[4] It bears mention that Pound's two-line poem—"The apparition of these faces in the crowd:/petals on a wet, black bough."—provide the novel's English-language title. While the Spanish *Los ingrávidos* [the weightless ones] places more emphasis on the spectral nature of the novel's protagonists, the English edition draws the reader immediately into this (intertextual) zone of contact across time and space.

[5] Luiselli was thinking in a variety of ways about the relationship between translation and space when she wrote this novel: her doctoral dissertation—titled, precisely, "Translation Spaces: Mexico City in the International Modernist Circuit" (2015)—seeks to define "a map of the physical and cultural spaces that foreigners and the foreign occupied in 1920s and 1930s Mexico City" (11) and examines the translation practice of none other than Gilberto Owen.

result, when we stumble upon the following passage, right around the midpoint of the novel—"En todas las novelas falta algo o alguien. Es esa novela no hay nadie. Nadie salvo un fantasma que a veces veía en el metro" (71) [All novels lack something or someone. In this novel there's no one. No one except a ghost that I used to see sometimes in the subway (69)]—and realize that the voice could plausibly belong to either character, we sense that we've been cast into an image of mutual literary creation reminiscent of a (subway) staircase drawn by M. C. Escher.

For anyone who has spent time with Jorge Luis Borges's "Pierre Menard, autor del Quijote" (1939) ["Pierre Menard, Author of the Quixote"], described by George Steiner as "the most acute, the most concentrated commentary anyone has offered on the business of translation" (1975: 73), it is hard not to think about the underground space of the subway in Luiselli's novel in relation to the "subterranean" project of that story's title character.[6] According to Borges's narrator, who is writing to set the record straight about the literary production of a recently deceased friend, Menard's oeuvre can be divided into his "visible" body of work and the "subterránea, la interminablemente heróica" one, "tal vez la más significativa de nuestro tiempo, consta de los capítulos noveno y trigésimo octavo de la primera parte del don Quijote y de un fragmento del capítulo veintidós" (2011: 111) [perhaps the most significant writing of our time, consists of the ninth and thirty-eighth chapters of Part I of *Don Quixote* and a fragment of Chapter XXII (1999: 90)].[7] Menard's visible work includes several translations from the Spanish, as well as a dizzying array of

---

[6] For more on this story and its relation to translation theory see Kristal 2002, Waisman 2005, and Arrojo 2018.

[7] The selections that comprise Menard's project are by no means arbitrary: they are moments when Cervantes asserts his novel's status as a translation or other form of re-writing. As Sergio Waisman observes: "Arguably the first modern novel, *Don Quijote* is structured as a story within a story, as a translation of various pre-texts. It is a rewriting of the chivalresque and picaresque novels, but also of an Arabic pre-text that exists only within the confines of the novel itself ... Cervantes's narrator finds Cide Hamete's manuscript in Toledo, a city ... with one of the most active and important schools of translation in Western history" (2005: 106–7).

philosophical monographs, invectives, and other intellectual ventures that share a remarkable tendency to contradict themselves, unraveling before the reader's eyes.[8] Beneath the surface, however, Menard is cultivating the "admirable ambition" not to translate Cervantes's canonical text or even to copy it, but instead to "producir unas páginas que coincidieran —palabra por palabra y línea por línea— con las de Miguel de Cervantes" (111) [produce a number of pages which coincided—word for word and line for line—with those of Miguel de Cervantes (91)]. The project, in this respect, is a resounding success: as the narrator notes, the two versions are "verbalmente idénticos" (115) [verbally identical (94)].

Beyond the philosophical questions surrounding *what*, precisely, Menard is doing when he talks about *producing* the *Quijote*—though the story has much to say about translation, it is important to point out that Menard's endeavor is not one, at least not in the interlingual sense—the radical gesture of this story resides in the retroactive effect that Menard's project has on the work it engages. In the same breath as he observes that the two texts are verbally identical, the narrator declares Menard's version to be "casi infinitamente más rico" (115) [almost infinitely richer (94)] due to the layers of meaning that arise from the recontextualization of the words centuries after their original appearance. One of the most memorable, and most frequently cited, moments of the story appears immediately after this praise: a close reading of two identical passages that presents Cervantes's reflection on truth and history as "mere rhetorical praise" of the latter, while the very same words from Menard's pen become a "staggering" and "brazenly pragmatic" idea.

Menard's subterranean project, however, is not simply an updated version that outshines or supplants the original: it actually

---

[8] For example, the "technical article on the possibility of enriching the game of chess by eliminating one of the rook's pawns," an idea that Menard "proposes, recommends, debates, and finally rejects," and the "diatribe against Paul Valéry" which "states the exact reverse of Menard's true opinion" (Borges 1999: 89–90).

reconstitutes it.[9] The narrator of the story concludes that "es lícito ver en el *Quijote* 'final' una especie de palimpsesto, en el que deben traslucirse los rastros —tenues pero no indescifrables— de la 'previa' escritura de nuestro amigo" (116) [it is legitimate to see the "final" Quixote as a kind of palimpsest, in which the traces—faint but not undecipherable— of our friend's "previous" text must shine through (95)]. It is here, above all, that the subterranean production of Pierre Menard meets the translational space of the subway in *Los ingrávidos*: in both cases, there is a reciprocal process of writing taking place backward and forward across time. In Luiselli's novel, one ghost writes the other into existence; in Borges's story, the trace of an endeavor that never saw the light of day leaves an indelible mark on the work that engendered it. The implications, moreover, of Menard's subterranean project extend beyond the denaturalization and revitalization of Cervantes's text; as Borges's narrator asserts, by way of conclusion:

> Menard (acaso sin quererlo) ha enriquecido mediante una técnica nueva el arte detenido y rudimentario de la lectura: la técnica del anacronismo deliberado y de las atribuciones erróneas. Esa técnica de aplicación infinita nos insta a recorrer la *Odisea* como si fuera posterior a la *Eneida* y el libro *Le jardin du Centaure* de madame Henri Bachelier como si fuera de madame Henri Bachelier.
>
> (2011: 117)

> Menard has (perhaps unwittingly) enriched the slow and rudimentary art of reading by means of a new technique—the technique of deliberate anachronism and fallacious attribution. That technique, requiring infinite patience and concentration, encourages us to read the *Odyssey* as though it came after the *Aeneid*, to read Mme. Henri Bachelier's *Le jardin du Centaure* as though it were written by Mme. Henri Bachelier.
>
> (1999: 95)

[9] According to Silviano Santiago, Menard's invisible work is "the paradox of the second text that completely disappears and thereby opens the space of its most evident signification: the cultural, social, and political situation in which the second author is located" (2001: 36). This invisibility is aligned, in Santiago's thought, with the Space In-between and the clandestinity through which the "anthropophagous ritual of Latin American discourse is constructed" (2001: 38).

In a characteristic gesture, Borges orients the entire story toward a poetics of reading that creates the text through imaginative, transgressive acts of (false) attribution. Anticipating Foucault's articulation of the author function by a quarter century, Borges mobilizes the frameworks imposed by biographical determinism toward dismantling precisely the fixity of the author sign and, with it, the idea that a text can "belong" to its author, whoever that might be.

Less frequently discussed, though it is key to the story's central conceit, is the fact that no record remains of Menard's endeavor: he destroyed his work as he produced it. Borges's narrator recounts that Menard wrote endless drafts, "corregió tenazmente y desgarró miles de páginas manuscritas. No permitió que fueran examinadas por nadie y cuidó que no le sobrevivieran.* En vano he procurado reconstruirlas" (2011: 116) [he stubbornly corrected, and he ripped up thousands of handwritten pages. He would allow no one to see them, and took care that they not survive him.* In vain have I attempted to reconstruct them (1999: 95)]. In the middle of this passage appears a footnote that describes the materiality of Menard's writing—the notebooks, the lettering—and the cheery bonfires it became. This materiality is all the more striking for the absence that follows: every trace of the work has been destroyed, and not even the friend who claims unique insight into the project is able to reconstruct his masterpiece.

The narrator of the story confesses at one point that, in the wake of Menard's intervention, he will never be able to read the Quixote the same way again. "¿Confesaré que suelo imaginar que la terminó y que leo el *Quijote*—todo el *Quijote*—como si lo hubiera pensado Menard?" (2011: 112) [Shall I confess that I often imagine that he did complete it, and that I read the Quixote—the *entire* Quixote—as if Menard had conceived it? (1999: 92)]. As such, I would argue that it is precisely its *invisibility*, its subterranean nature, that endows Menard's project with its power. Because its limits are so hard to define, it can be everywhere and nowhere at once; transforming, retroactively, the version penned by Cervantes.

Along these same lines, the novels of this chapter foreground the "scene" of translation not only in the sense of a narrative staging, but also that of a locus or site of activity. The chapter's title not only posits translation as an act of writing in a territory where invisibility and marginality in the negative sense are transformed into a freedom from the restrictions imposed on the visible world; it also suggests a dismissal of sorts—a "writing off" in the sense of a willingness to leave geopolitical demarcations, and the inequities that attend them, behind. Just as the space allotted the translator at the lower margin of the page both attests to the subordinate position traditionally assigned to translation and provides a site for the subversion of this hierarchical relation, the physical spaces occupied by translator protagonists in the novels discussed in this chapter both foreground and interrogate the uneven distribution of cultural capital established along national-literary lines.

I. Carpet and Fringe

From a false translation that has real effects on its author's professional and spatio-temporal position, to translators who convene at the end of the world and others tucked so deeply into the corners of their respective milieux that they are almost imperceptible, or the setting of a translational love affair described as a "moving city" impossible to pin down, formulations of the translator's "place" in the world abound in contemporary Latin American fiction.[10] I was not surprised to find this wide range of material to draw from, given how central

---

[10] Andrés Neuman's *El viajero del siglo* (2009) [*Traveler of the Century* trans. Nick Caistor and Lorenza Garcia 2012], though not discussed in this chapter, is another novel that engages spatial metaphors in its *mise en scène* of translation. The action of the novel unfolds against the backdrop of a place called Wandernburg (from the German verb *wandern*, expressing mobility, peregrination), which is described in the epigraph as a "ciudad móvil sit. aprox. entre los ant. est. de Sajonia y Prusia. Cap. del ant. principado del m. nombre. Lat. N y long. E indefinidas por desplazamiento," the exact location of which remains unknown, despite reports from travelers.

spatial metaphors are to the discussion of translation, theoretically and anecdotally. As Michael Emmerich has observed,

> translation is often described as a "bridge" between languages, cultures, nations. Both the notion of translation as something that takes place in an "in-between" place and the particular metaphor of the bridge are so common, and cleave so well to both the etymology of the word "translation" itself and to the spatial metaphors we use when we speak of translation (again: we translate *from* one language *into* another), that at times it seems impossible to think of translation in any other way.
>
> (2013: 49)

In Romance languages and English alike, the term "translation" is linked to the Latin *translatio*, which means both translation and transfer.[11] That this etymology connects it to the concept of *translatio imperii et studii*, by which knowledge and (the exercise of) power radiate outward from a single hegemonic point of origin, is not without relevance to the present study: translation has long been an intrinsic part of global, as well as cultural, politics and we continue to conceive of it along those lines.

In "Taking Fidelity Philosophically," Barbara Johnson carries this metaphor a step further, arguing that translation "is a bridge that creates out of itself the two fields of battle it separates" (1985: 148). The space of translation is thus imbued with a double agency: not only does it create a zone of contact between two existing (cultural and/or political) fields, it constitutes the fields themselves. In practical terms, we know this to be true: on one hand, translated works reconfigure the literary landscape in which they appear by expanding its range of perspectives and aesthetics; on the other, the original work is itself reconfigured by the readings produced in this new context.[12] Johnson's characterization of these cultural fields as "fields of battle," moreover,

---

[11] There is, of course, also the German *übersetzen*, which appears extensively in (Western) canonical translation theory and means to "place" something "over or across."

[12] This is to say nothing of instances of diplomatic interpretation or the interlingual negotiation of trade agreements, or similar instances of translation, which represent a literal extreme of Johnson's formulation.

draws attention to the ideological struggles that underlie even the most apparently smooth instances of literary transfer: which works are selected to circulate in another language, which preconceptions are reinforced or challenged, which political dynamics exist between the languages and literary systems in question, which aesthetic criteria are imposed or effaced in the process of transmission; the list goes on. Even when translation is undertaken in the spirit of welcoming a voice into a new literary context—as it so often is—it will always be inflected with the politics of the cultural backdrop against which it occurs.

This formulation of translation as a site of conflict is also central to one of the more polemical reflections on World Literature to appear at the turn of the millennium, the same moment as most of the works included in this study. In *The World Republic of Letters* (1999) Pascale Casanova presents translation as a motor of literary "consecration and excommunication" (2004: 20); in the struggle for what she describes as cultural legitimacy, it "constitutes the principal means of access to the literary world for all writers outside the center" and subsequently represents "a major prize and weapon in international literary competition" (133). In this account, translation is both a "celebration" and an "annexation" (154), and its agents hold the strings of the cultural bourse at the same time they are subject to the hierarchical structures of cultural geopolitics.

Casanova's study, which aimed to shift the scope of analysis from the individual literary work to the interaction of literary worlds, revealing what Henry James has called the "figure in the carpet," is among many works of criticism that apply Emmanuel Wallerstein's world-system economic model—according to which all production belongs to a unified but unequal system composed of a center, a periphery, and a semi-periphery—to the dynamics of cultural exchange.[13] Here,

---

[13] Casanova cites Fernand Braudel, Henry James, and Valery Larbaud as her primary influences, but the structural presence of Wallerstein's model is unmistakable in the concept of the "Greenwich Meridian" of literature and the relationship of dominating and dominated literatures. Moretti, on the other hand, does cite Wallerstein as an influence (Moretti 2000: 57).

too, metaphors of mapping abound: Casanova examines the rivalries among what she repeatedly describes as dominated and dominating languages in terms of the "irremediable and violent discontinuity between the metropolitan literary world and its suburban outskirts" (43).

Though Casanova recognizes the complexity of the translator's role in this process of cultural exchange, her analysis is irremediably bound to a hierarchical, unidirectional notion of cultural influence, as evidenced by the highly normative structuring principle of the "Greenwich meridian" of literature. According to the French scholar, the literatures of so-called "dominated" languages are defined—to varying degrees—as "belated" relative to models established in the metropolis, which just happens to be essentially coextensive with Paris.[14] Borges, because he won the approval of a French readership, is an "exceptional figure" within a "destitute literary space … very far from the Greenwich meridian" (280).

One can imagine Borges's biting retort. Better yet, we don't need to imagine it, as he articulated his thoughts on the matter quite clearly in a 1951 talk presented at the Colegio Libre de Estudios Superiores in Buenos Aires. In "El escritor argentino y la tradición" ["The Argentine Writer and Tradition"], Borges celebrates the fact that Argentina falls outside the gravitational center of Western culture, as this peripheral position implies the critical distance necessary for innovation. Addressing the question of what tradition Argentinian writers can claim, by way of a reflection on their Jewish and Irish peers—who, he argues, act within a culture and yet "no se sienten atados a ella por una devoción especial" (1997a: 200) [do not feel bound to it by any special devotion (2000: 426)]—Borges asserts:

---

[14] For an elegant series of critical responses to this premise, see Ignacio Sánchez Prado's edited volume *América Latina en la "literatura mundial"* (2006).

Creo que nuestra tradición es toda la cultura occidental, y creo también que tenemos derecho a esta tradición, mayor que el que pueden tener los habitantes de una u otra nación occidental ... podemos manejar todos los temas europeos, manejarlos sin supersticiones, con una irreverencia que puede tener, y ya tiene, consecuencias afortunadas.

(200–1)

I believe that our tradition is the whole of Western culture, and I also believe that we have a right to this tradition, a greater right than that which the inhabitants of one Western nation or another may have ... we can take on all the European subjects, take them on without superstition and with an irreverence than can have, and already has had, fortunate consequences.

(426)

Anticipating and forestalling the notion that metropolitan centers of culture are fires whose warmth writers at the "periphery" jostle to absorb, grateful for the respite from the cold wasteland of their own natural environments, Borges insists on the power to be found in the irreverence at the margins, in the corners, out of sight.[15] Like the Latin American writers in Borges's formulation, the translator protagonists of the novels that follow—both centrally important and marginalized, both a conduit and a point of friction in the global circulation of cultural goods—offer a challenge to the paired notions of property and propriety from their place both on and off the map of cultural exchange that they themselves make possible.

---

[15] In this sense, the subterranean space in which Pierre Menard produces his masterpiece anticipates Borges's remarks in "El escritor argentino y la traducción." Another (spatialized) point of contact between the two texts is the rejection of "local color" found in both: the story's narrator approvingly observes that Menard "Desatiende o proscribe el color local. Ese desdén indica un sentido nuevo de la novela histórica" (2011: 114) [He ignores, overlooks—or banishes—local color. That disdain posits a new meaning for the "historical novel" (1999: 93)]. Similarly, the complementary line of argumentation to the passage cited above in "El escritor argentino y la tradición" invites the Argentinean writer to eschew local themes (his most pointed criticism is directed at the gauchesque) because, on one hand, they are just as artificial as any other possible topic, and on the other, because they do not make a work any more authentic (here, he observes that no one doubts the authenticity of the Quran, despite the lack of camels roaming its verses).

II. Quite a View You've Got Here

One thing that is particularly striking about these novels that open alternative or invisible spaces for their translator protagonists is the consistency with which this unmappability dovetails with a foregrounding of market and labor conditions. Though the translational space of the subway in Valeria Luiselli's *Los ingrávidos* seems to generate zones of contact that eschew familiar conceptions of place and time, the novel is situated very firmly in the known world of cultural markets: the genesis of the young woman's literary forgery is the imperative (imposed by her employer, White, who stands in for the publishing industry more broadly) to make Owen's story appeal to anglophone readers.[16]

Pablo De Santis's *La traducción* (1998) [The translation], which is discussed in Chapter 2, likewise creates a translational non-space as a zone of contact, while it connects the translator's invisibility to their paradoxical position at both the margins and the center of the cultural and economic systems to which they belong. As mentioned earlier, the novel centers on a series of mysterious deaths at a translators' conference in the coastal town of Puerto Esfinge, or Port Sphinx. In addition to its name, which evokes the mysteries and hermeneutic machinations of both the deaths and the translations that take place there, the town is shown from the outset as being in a state of ruin—as in Benesdra's *El traductor* (1998) [The translator], a nod to the failed neoliberal policies of Carlos Menem. After entering the city limits, the first thing to appear is a cemetery, followed by an abandoned lighthouse. As for the hotel where the conference is to be held, it is:

> totalmente desproporcionado en comparación con Puerto Esfinge. Era el centro de un gran complejo turístico que no había llegado a existir ... Una mitad estaba terminada y empezaba a decaer; la otra mitad no tenía puertas, ni ventanas ni mampostería. Un cartel inmenso

---

[16] The difference among literary markets also plays out in the history of the novel itself: when Luiselli's novel was translated into English, Louis Zukofsky was translated as/into Joshua Zvorsky, and the title of his epic objectivist poem was also changed—a concession to the new juridical context into which the book was to be inserted.

anunciaba la continuación de las obras, pero no se veían maquinarias ni obreros ni materiales de construcción.

(21)

totally disproportionate to the town of Puerto Esfinge. It was the center of a vast tourist complex that never came to be … half of it was finished and was already beginning to crumble; the other half had no doors, windows or drywall. A huge sign announced the ongoing construction, but there were no machines, workers, or materials anywhere in sight.

Puerto Esfinge's dilapidated hotel stands empty precisely because it sits outside the regular circuits of goods and tourism: despite the optimistic development plans that predicted otherwise, the town is invisible from an economic standpoint. This invisibility (as well as its tenuous financial situation) mirrors and serves as a commentary on the translators who inhabit it, albeit temporarily—principally but not exclusively De Blast, who is described by his lover as "el hombre invisible" (32) [the invisible man] in a clear reference to the linked processes of erasure and self-effacement so intrinsic to the experience of a translator. The isolation and precarity of this space are underscored from the outset of the novel. During the long trip from the nearest airport to the site of the conference, De Blast observes that the other passengers:

> comentaban el paisaje, es decir, el no-paisaje. A los costados del camino no había nada … [Rina] sacó de la cartera un plano y lo desplegó con alguna dificultad. Los mapas son una versión abstracta del paisaje; pero en aquel viaje las cosas ocurrían al revés, y el paisaje era una versión abstracta del mapa. Me señaló un punto junto al mar. Busqué el nombre del pueblo, pero no lo encontré.

(20)

> discussed the landscape, that is, the non-landscape. There was nothing on either side of the road … [Rina] pulled a map out of her purse and unfolded it, with some difficulty. Maps are an abstract version of the landscape, but everything was backwards on that trip, and the landscape was an abstract version of the map. She pointed to a spot by the sea. I looked for the name of the town but couldn't find it.

It almost sounds like the beginning of an uninteresting joke, this busload of translators heading toward an invisible destination through a landscape described as "an abstract version" of the map one of them holds in his hands. But like all jokes it has a serious side, starting with the adjective "abstract," which can here be taken not only in the sense of being almost unrecognizable—though it certainly suggests that— but also in its etymological sense: the word is derived from *abstrahere*, meaning to take away, set free, or to separate. Puerto Esfinge does not belong to the same topological system as its surroundings.

Another work that presents its translator protagonist as occupying a marginal, nearly invisible space is César Aira's *La Princesa Primavera* (2003) [Princess Springtime]. Even more than *La traducción*, the novel insists on the intersection of the cultural and economic dynamics that attend the circulation of texts as goods—in this case, escapist commercial fiction published in pirate editions with no regard for intellectual property law. The translator protagonist from whom the novel draws its name lives on an "islita perdida" (60) [secluded little island][17] caught between participation in and isolation from the global market: basic supplies and texts to translate reach her, but the virtually uninhabited island operates largely on a barter economy and as such is insulated from the market dynamics outlined above. The princess makes barely any money for the translations of commercial fiction she is assigned—"eso está demás decirlo" (14) [that goes without saying], Aira quips—but what she does earn meets her modest needs.

Though the island is described as being off the coast of Panama, and though the business practices of the publishing houses for which the princess translates are explicitly grounded in the economic dynamics of the industry in Latin America (reference is made to distribution channels running from Mexico to Argentina, for example), its diminutive size and hybrid internal economy situate the island at least partially off the map of global networks of cultural and financial exchange. This is, of course, until the narrative unfolds

---

[17] The literal translation would be "lost little island."

in typical Airan fashion, with the arrival of the fearsome General Invierno [General Winter] who, along with his lieutenant, Arbolito de Navidad [Christmas Tree], wants to annex the island for Siberia. Our protagonist is distracted from her labor for most of the novel as she deals with the intruders, but (after another characteristically Airan *deus ex machina* denouement) is ultimately able to return to her desk and set herself a more aggressive, but entirely achievable, goal of pages translated per day to get herself back on track and preserve her reputation as a reliable worker.

As we saw in Chapter 1, translation is a recurring theme in César Aira's fiction; in *La Princesa Primavera*, he reflects extensively on translation as a profession, borrowing from his own experience as a translator of best-sellers.[18] In addition to an extensive reflection on the way translators' labor is exploited in the name of cost reduction, Aira posits two distinct ways invisibility and the physical space occupied by the translator relate to these structures of power. Speaking generally about the reception of translations, he claims most people believe that "la traducción era tanto mejor cuanto más invisible. Y la gran mayoría de los lectores, por no decir todos, en especial tratándose de esa clase de novelas, directamente ignoraba que hubiera un traductor" (16) [the more invisible the translation, the better. Most readers, if not all, and especially of this kind of novel, had no idea there even was a translator]. Though she takes great pride in her work, and though she is sought out by publishers for her speed and accuracy, no one else seems aware she's there at all.

Princess Springtime's invisibility is tempered by the fact that she lives and works in a marginal space with some pretty extraordinary views: the top of one of the palace's towers, which houses her sun-drenched office and its extensive library.[19] She also spends time on the tower's

---

[18] In the interview mentioned earlier, Aira discusses the years he spent translating best-sellers because "los editores pagan lo mismo por la mala que por la buena, y la buena es mucho más difícil de traducir" (Duarte 2009: np) [editors pay the same for bad literature as good, and good literature is much harder to translate].

[19] This tower lined with books evokes both that of Babel and the fiction of Borges.

walkways, the space that most explicitly associates scopic privilege with power. Aira writes that if she wanted to "dominar el panorama completo en todo el círculo del horizonte no tenía más que subir a las torres, con una de las cuales, la más alta de ese lado del edificio, tenía comunicación directa desde sus compartimentos" (10) [dominate the entire panorama around the entire circle of the horizon, all she had to do was climb up to the towers, one of which, the tallest on that side of the building, connected directly with her rooms]. Though one cannot help but wonder what exactly is meant by "dominar" in this case, what is clear is that Aira is positing a privileged vantage point as part of his translator protagonist's identity.

This detail takes on greater significance in light of Aira's choice to have his translator protagonist dedicate her professional energies to formulaic best-sellers. In a gesture similar to his unorthodox presentation in *El congreso de literatura* of cloning not as a conservative model of faithful reproduction but as a motor of creative infidelity, in *La Princesa Primavera* Aira presents the translation of commercial fiction, itself marginalized within critical discourse, as a space within which the distribution of authority between author and translator can be destabilized. In a soft justification of the total disregard for intellectual property law exercised by her employers, who publish pirate editions of these bestsellers, our translator protagonist reflects:

> ¿Y quiénes eran los autores? Cada volumen tenía un nombre y un apellido en la tapa y en la portada, pero eso era todo. Un nombre intercambiable por cualquier otro, de hombre o de mujer, lo mismo daba. Pero en la novela misma no había autor, es decir estilo, obra, casillero en la historia de la literatura. Eran simplemente productos ... Por algunos datos encontrados en las solapas, la Princesa había sospechado que muchos de los nombres que precedían al título eran seudónimos ... en otros casos, se traslucía una escritura colectiva, de tipo "línea de montaje". De modo que daba lo mismo que fueran anónimas ... Otra cosa (lo contrario) era el trabajo que se tomaba ella por hacer traducciones fieles ... en una prosa elegante y fluida, sin regionalismos.
>
> (26–7)

And who were the authors? Every volume had a first and last name on the cover and title page, but that was all. A name that was interchangeable with any other, man's or woman's, it didn't matter. In the novel itself, though, there was no author—that is, style, oeuvre, place in literary history. They were simply products ... Certain details included on the book's flaps made the Princess suspect that many of the names that came before the title were pseudonyms ... in other cases, she could sense more than one person writing, a kind of "assembly line." So it would have been just the same if the novels had been anonymous. It was a different matter (the complete opposite), the effort she put into translating faithfully ... in elegant, fluent prose free of regionalisms.

There's a lot going on here, starting with the emptying out of the author sign, which is no longer a reliable indicator of who actually wrote the book (one outcome of the need to generate an unending stream of *products* to meet market demand). It is also irrelevant, because there is nothing contained within the volume's pages worth connecting to an oeuvre or, as Aira says, inserting into literary history. In this way, the author becomes just as invisible as the translator—perhaps even more so, since a trained eye would be able to detect the difference between Princess Springtime's carefully wrought translations and the sloppy ones produced by her colleagues. Especially noteworthy is the fact that what makes her translations so sought after is the absence of regionalisms in her prose. That is, its resistance to being situated on the map of the diverse Spanishes that exist around the world, ideal from a practical perspective because this makes it easier for the same translation to circulate in different markets, but also significant in that it creates the category of an invisible *linguistic* space.

The fact that Aira lists, among the virtues of the Princess's prose, that it is elegant and fluent also establishes a connection with the "cult of fluency" that, according to Lawrence Venuti, not only creates the "illusion of authorial presence" (1995: 381), but also points "to the violence that resides in the very purpose and activity of translation: the reconstitution of the foreign text in accordance with values, beliefs and representations that preexist it in the target language, always configured in hierarchies of dominance and marginality, always determining the production, circulation, and reception of texts" (18). In other words, the framing—by editors who aggressively standardize syntax; by publishers who omit the translator's name from the book's cover and marketing materials; by reviewers who neglect to name the translator—of a translated text as though it had been written in the target language effaces not only the creative intervention of the person who in fact strung those words together, but also the numerous politically charged interventions inherent to any text's passage from one language to another, imposing a new set of aesthetic and ideological coordinates upon the work.

The explicit critique of late capitalism and the alienation of intellectual labor seen in *La Princesa Primavera* is even more marked in Salvador Benesdra's *El traductor* (1998), in which the translator's invisibility is explored in terms of his role in the publishing industry and the physical space he occupies in the world. The novel appears in Chapter 2 of this study, but in the interest of refreshing our memory: its protagonist, Ricardo Zevi, is a translator working on staff at a left-leaning publishing house called Turba, which is in the process of being absorbed by a multinational media conglomerate at the height of the neoliberal frenzy in Argentina that led, in the years following the novel's publication, to a massive economic crisis. This transition brings with it all manner of editorial and organizational upheaval; Turba's attempt to enter—or its capitulation to—the global marketplace brings with it considerable anxiety, much of which is tied to the idea of placelessness: massive layoffs are made to trim the bottom line, and although Zevi is able to keep his job, he finds that he is being pushed further and further toward the margins of the company.

It is worth noting that both the firings and Zevi's shrinking role within Turba are described as displacements or "desubicaciones" in the text, calling attention to the intersection of power—here, discursive authority and economic influence overlap—and the spaces assigned to those who operate under its sway.[20] The marginalization of both Ricardo Zevi and the small publisher for whom he works depicted in the novel, then, is a concrete reminder of the ways in which the biases and predilections of a handful of nations exert a formative effect on the international life of a text and, indeed, of the echoes of colonial domination that mark a publishing industry shaped by a handful of major conglomerates localized in metropolitan centers of economic power. And yet, though Turba's position in this hierarchical system leaves it subject to the aesthetic and ideological incursions of its new parent company, *El traductor* offers an image of this marginality— and, indeed, of translational invisibility—that suggests its own form of empowerment.

Benesdra situates Zevi in a unique, and uniquely fitting, apartment in the cupola of an old building. In so doing, he presents the fundamental paradox of translation in spatial terms: though Zevi is subject to the hierarchical dynamics of global commerce and cultural exchange as a professional occupying a specific site in the World Republic of Letters, some part of him exists in a space not contained by this system; from there, he has the potential to exert a destabilizing force upon it. Citing a decades-old obsession with finding just such an apartment, Zevi homes in on the fundamental *inscrutability* of his domicile. "No puedo ver el cielo por el techo," Benesdra writes, "pero veo más crepúsculos que el Principito. Y no creo que la gente se imagine que aquí vive alguien. Es como un periscopio espiando la ciudad" (1998: 80) [I can't see the sky because of the ceiling, but I see more twilights than the Little Prince. I don't think anyone would guess someone lives here. It's like a periscope pointed at the city].

Immediately notable here is the privileged gaze from the periphery. Ensconced in his "periscope," Zevi is able to observe the city from an

---

[20] In Spanish, particularly in Argentina, to be "desubicado" is also to be *out of line*, that is, to refuse to act according to one's assigned place in a given milieu. Similarly, "ubicarse" or to locate oneself, refers to a variety of conceptual, social, and spatial orientations. All these layers of meaning intersect with the notion of propriety, and all are present in Benesdra's choice of the term.

angle at which it is rarely seen. This is not a panoptic form of observation, however, in that its power is not derived from the internalization of the authority of a central locus of surveillance. Quite the opposite: the privilege of this space is precisely its position both on and off the map of the city. This unmappability is reinforced by Zevi's comment that, though he can't see the sky from his apartment, he is instead treated to "more *crepúsculos* than the Little Prince." Rather than observing the course of the sun through the heavens, or the constellations (before GPS or Google Maps, the primary means of establishing one's geographic location), Zevi's skyscape consists of the *intermediary*, that time *between* day and night. The use of the term "crepúsculo" is also key here: while being the moment-in-between that allows day and night to exist as distinct entities, the term is not tethered to a single meaning: in Spanish, *crepúsculo* is used for both dawn and dusk, each of which have an alternate translation that would situate them more specifically.

All three of the novels examined above, then, posit a direct connection between the physical space occupied by their translator protagonists and their condition of cultural invisibility. While for De Santis the invisibility and marginality of Puerto Esfinge is a spatial manifestation of the invisibility and marginality of the translator within the literary system, Aira and Benesdra attach a positive valence to this invisibility; in both cases, this positive valence is tied to the translators occupying a space from which they can see without being seen, act from within a space not situated on the map. For Aira, the privileged vantage point of a tower located on a nearly invisible island dovetails with the freedom of working with texts not considered literary, that neither fit the model of the author sign nor operate according to the laws of intellectual property; for Benesdra, the possibility of glimpsing the intermediary from a perspective few others share, is both a physicalization of translation and a statement of its promise. Though all three of these translators are subject to the hierarchical dynamics of global commerce and cultural exchange as professionals occupying a subordinate place in the World Republic of Letters, some part of them exists in a space not (de)limited by this system.

III. Into the Woods

Few writers center the question of situatedness as explicitly in their work, or tie it as compellingly to an ethics of writing and translation, as Cristina Rivera Garza, author of more than a dozen books and the only two-time winner of the prestigious Sor Juana Inés de la Cruz Prize. For Rivera Garza, who both translates and engages questions of transmission and intelligibility extensively in her fiction and criticism, "translation brings up dissent, discordance, deviation, contention" and always involves "issues of power" (2019: np). These ideas also inform her writing practice. In the same interview, Rivera Garza observes:

> Marc Auge made an argument not too long ago about the no-places we are prone to inhabit. This, which may be read as a displacement of place, has, in fact, emphasized the tentative, provisional, at times impersonal nature of place in our contemporary world. I tend to think less about space as such and more about territory (space plus politics). Just as I write from and through a body—a body among bodies—I do so in territories linked by economic inequality and cultural diversity. Am I addressing the question of accumulation? This is what I ask of my writing process. Am I attentive enough to issues of territory and embodiment?

(2019: np)

There is an important difference between the territories here invoked, which represent the intersection of multiple subjective spaces and power dynamics, and hierarchical relations that define the map of national literatures described by Casanova, tied as it is to a set of privileges and prejudices. The associated focus on the body as site of enunciation is certainly prominent in Rivera Garza's 2012 novel *El mal de la taiga* [*The Taiga Syndrome* trans. Suzanne Jill Levine and Aviva Kana 2018], as is the insistence on the intersection of place and politics.

The narrator of *El mal de la taiga* is a former detective who retired after chalking up more failures than closed cases and turned to writing fictionalized accounts of some of these loose ends for a "small but prestigious press" (2018: 21). She is approached at a party one night by a wealthy individual and hired to track down his second wife, who has run off with another man into the dense forest of the Taiga.[21] Our narrator accepts the assignment and, in turn, enlists the services of a translator to help her as she moves further into the uncharted territory of the forest. Though this individual acts as an exclusively oral mediator, it is worth noting that he is identified throughout as a "traductor" (translator) rather than an "intérprete" (interpreter); this gesture subtly reinforces the sensation that the world through which the two are moving is at once located on the global map of natural resource exploitation and in a mythical, intertextual realm.[22]

The space in which these translational operations take place is explicitly presented as the "deep dark wood" of fairy tales: the missing woman and her lover are described repeatedly as Hansel and Gretel, while the narrator has visions of red capes, red threads, and a wolf that eventually attacks. It is also a space that has been carved up by the scythe of the lumber industry: the town at the edge of the forest that both the fleeing couple and the pair on their trail use as a temporary base camp is organized completely around logging and its ancillary usurers, provisioners, and sex shops. In this way, the Taiga, despite being described several times as the "world's end" or "fin del mundo," is nonetheless a politicized territory in the sense outlined above.

The narrator first meets the translator in the airport of a "ciudad fronteriza" (2012: 38) or "border city" (2018: 35) that divides the known world from this "world's end"—a space of circulation situated at a limit, congruent with the translator's embodied practice of crossing back and forth between languages and cultures:

---

[21] "Taiga" is capitalized in the English translation, a gesture I will preserve here.
[22] As mentioned earlier, another translation narrative that features an interpreter set against an unstable map is Pedro Mairal's El año del desierto (2005), in which a multilingual corporate secretary named María Neyla Valdén bears witness to the un-making of the nation as Buenos Aires slips back in time toward its origins as a small port city at the outer edge of a hostile wilderness. As the narrative progresses, both the space of "civilization" and the physical disposition of the city correspond to maps of the territory dating further and further back in time. For more on this novel and its connection to Argentina's 2001 economic crisis, see Zimmer 2013.

Si no hubiera estado al tanto de sus varios empleos en buques de pesca o en áreas de producción de madera dentro del bosque o en el mundo de la caza, habría pensado que se trataba de un hombre frágil. El primer saludo me había permitido constatar la piel rugosa de la yema de los dedos y las palmas de la mano ... —Yo vengo de allá — me dijo, señalando un lugar indeterminado que hube que imaginar como la taiga.

(2012: 39–40)

If I had not been aware of his hunting experience and his various jobs on fishing boats and in the lumber industry, I might have thought he was a fragile man. When he shook my hand, I could feel the coarse skin of his palms and the rough tips of his fingers ... "I come from over there," he told me, pointing out a vague area on the horizon that I had to imagine was the Taiga.

(2018: 36–7)

This confusion regarding the translator's origins is redoubled toward the end of the novel, after their mission has failed and the narrator is about to make her way home without the woman who had fled from her husband. In the same airport, in a moment symmetrically joined to this first encounter, reproduced above, he tells the narrator that he had been born on an oil rig built in the middle of a lake, that the place in many ways had determined his trajectory. When the narrator asks whether he hadn't said he was from the Taiga, he replies, "Claro, de ahí. Sí" (107) [Yes ... from over there, exactly (109)]; and the narrator assumes that she simply hadn't understood. The translator, then, comes from the dark wood and/or an oil rig set up in the middle of a lake: it is not only the place itself that defines his course, but also the instability that underlies it, in a state of flux or indeterminacy between conjunction and exclusion. Despite the abstraction of the geographic location from which he hails, in both the description of the location and that of his physical appearance, marked by manual labor conditioned by the area in which he was raised, the translator's body is joined from the outset to the violence of extraction and the machinations of international markets.

In the same way Rivera Garza tenaciously emphasizes the physicality of the translator in the passage above, acts of enunciation and translation are also systematically endowed with a material presence—not only in the moment of transmission, which occurs in the time of the narrative, but also projected into the future, as the narrator anticipates reporting back to her client and explaining to him the clues received through these layers of mediation.

> Le diría, por ejemplo, que cuando yo escribiera: "Les pregunté si tenían electricidad y ellos me respondieron mostrándome una vela encendida", debía considerar que la pregunta la había enunciado yo, en efecto, pero que antes de recibir la respuesta, que tardó en llegar, el traductor tuvo que hacerme repetir la pregunta un par de veces y, luego, tuvo que enunciarla él también un par de veces hasta que los habitantes de la comarca de la última taiga pudieron entenderla y, a su vez, contestarla.
>
> (2012: 37)

> I would tell him—for example, when I wrote: "I asked if they had electricity and they responded by showing me a lit candle"—that he should realize I had, in fact, pronounced that question, but before I received the answer, which came much later, the translator had made me repeat the question several times, and then had said it several times himself until the inhabitants of the village in the Taiga could understand it and answer.
>
> (2018: 34–5)

The translator, here and everywhere, is both a vehicle of transmission but also a site of friction: the assumption of smooth interlinguistic transfer upon which global commerce depends is shown here to be, in fact, a laborious and not entirely reliable process. The rhythm of this passage, especially in the Spanish, reinforces the sensation that we are pressing our way through the Taiga itself, a dense forest of language.[23]

---

[23] As spatial metaphors for translation go, this image—and the entire setting of the novel, in fact—recall Walter Benjamin's "language forest" in "The Task of the Translator" (1923), as described in Chapter 2. "Unlike a work of literature," Benjamin writes, "translation does not find itself in the center of the language forest but on the outside facing the wooded ridge; it calls into it without entering, aiming at that single spot where the echo is able to give, in its own language, the reverberation of the work in the alien one" (Benjamin 2005: 258–9).

This foundational moment when the two characters meet for the first time, appears in a chapter titled "Algo de su lengua en mi lengua" in Spanish (literally, "some/thing of [his] tongue in/on mine") and "Tongue to Tongue" in English. Though each emphasizes these elements to varying degrees and with slightly different nuances, both versions underscore the physicality of language, erotic contact, and—particularly in the Spanish—contamination. In the Spanish, as well, the tongue/language becomes a territory in its own right, one on which something can be located. The interaction itself proves even more complex, creating a new linguistic territory from the contact between the first two.

> Algo dijo en mi lengua pero, al darse cuenta de que lo entendía sólo con dificultad, optó por usar la lengua en la que hablaríamos durante el trayecto a los bosques boreales: algo que no era estrictamente suyo ni mío, un tercer espacio, una segunda lengua común.
>
> (2012: 39)

> He said something in my language but upon realizing that I had difficulty understanding, he chose to use the language that we would speak during our journey through the boreal forest: a language that was not strictly his nor mine, a third space, a second tongue in common.
>
> (2018: 36)

The translator tries, at first, to "cross over" into the narrator's language; then, understanding that she can't speak his own, shifts into a tongue described as a *third space*, a formulation that evokes Homi Bhabha's concept of the same name. According to Bhabha,

> The intervention of the Third Space of enunciation, which makes the structure of meaning and reference an ambivalent process ... challenges our sense of the historical identity of culture as a homogenizing, unifying force, authenticated by the originary Past ... It is that Third Space, though unrepresentable in itself, which constitutes the discursive conditions of enunciation that ensure that the meaning and symbols of culture have no primordial unity or fixity; that even the same signs can be appropriated, translated, rehistoricized, and read anew.
>
> (2004: 54–5)

This Third Space opened up by the translator in Rivera Garza's narrative, then, not only creates a zone of contact between languages and experiences, it redraws the unidirectional flows of influence characteristic of traditional cultural geopolitics as a multidimensional, trans-historical network of creative appropriation and reimagination.[24] The discursive power consolidated in the "originary Past" of a privileged source text is thus shattered and redistributed, allowed to interact in previously unthinkable ways. Most importantly, the flow becomes reciprocal: the same work that "influences" another is also reconstituted by the contact.

In this reciprocity, Bhabha's concept resonates with the creative re-writing embodied by the figure of Pierre Menard, author of an (invisible) engagement of the *Quixote* that changed forever the way the work is read, who "(acaso sin quererlo) ha enriquecido mediante una técnica nueva el arte detenido y rudimentario de la lectura: la técnica del anacronismo deliberado y de las atribuciones erróneas" (Borges 2011: 117) [(perhaps unwittingly) enriched the slow and rudimentary art of reading by means of a new technique—the technique of deliberate anachronism and fallacious attribution (Borges 1999: 95)].

Situated in this Third Space, engaging this subterranean work, reading and (re-)writing at the periphery, the contemporary writer-translators discussed in this chapter join Menard in asserting that "todo hombre debe ser capaz de todas las ideas y entiendo que en el porvenir lo será" (2011: 117) [every man should be capable of all ideas, and I believe that in the future he shall be (1999: 95)]. Even as they engage the dynamics of an international literary market they observe up close, in all its inequality and geopolitical specificity, they are also insisting on a critical space apart, unseen and unmappable, from which to upturn

---

[24] In this sense, the Third Space is aligned with Santiago's concept of the Space In-between: both are unrepresentable, and both, from their space of invisibility, reconstitute the works and traditions they engage.

the notion of intellectual property and the cult of the original, upon which so many vertical relationships of discursive and economic power depend.

Ultimately, just as the marginal textual space of the footnote complicates and undermines the monologic authority of the body text, the marginal physical spaces occupied by these translator protagonists allow them to operate both within and outside the hierarchical organization of nationally grounded networks of cultural exchange of which they form a conflicted part. These representations of translational space operate as a positive appropriation of the qualities of invisibility and marginality to undermine, structurally, the hierarchies of cultural geopolitics as they are traditionally understood. In subterranean spaces and unseen corners, it is not the privileged figure of authorial genius but rather the everyday, everywhere acts of reading and re-imagining that confer meaning, in the most vital terms.

Coda: Reading for Distance

This is not the coda I was planning to write. That I did write, that sits written. That other coda was or is about possible futures for the literary representation of the translator in the digital age, given both the ways technological advancements have changed the capacity of computer-assisted and machine translation, and the ways in which the idea of intellectual property is being challenged by both the digital commons and practices of remixing that refute the notion of unitary authorship. Like Bellatin's phantom footnote on Kawabata, that other coda probably haunts these remarks, but the fact is that, when thinking about possible futures, I found myself drawn overwhelmingly to the analog.

What I most wanted to communicate in that other coda was the way translation narratives, by nature, present an inherently collaborative model of authorship that challenges the strictures of intellectual property; I wanted to talk about the way these narratives insist on understanding the text as something created anew with each interpretive iteration. Still, as much as I wanted to see all that in interactive media projects and literary remixes—and did, in many—my mind kept returning to the classroom, and to the practice of *distancing* reading proposed by the novels here studied.[1]

The attempt to bring a decentralized concept of authorship and an ethics of reading into the classroom takes two principal forms for

---

[1] This distancing form of reading invokes but runs contrary to Moretti's proposal of *distant* reading, insofar as it seeks not to take vast swaths of literature as a single unit of analysis, but rather to create an ethical engagement with the translated work by protecting its specificity—the distance from which we observe it even within the target literary system. It also differs from Venuti's call for foreignizing translations. For more on these distinctions, see Chapter 2, "Foreign Correspondence."

me. The first is a sustained discussion of the interventions that go into putting a translated book in the students' hands; the second is a series of creative and critical exercises that show them firsthand the kinds of choices that go into every translation. For thinking broadly about these questions, Lawrence Venuti's "Translation and the Pedagogy of Literature," together with "How to Read a Translation," are excellent resources for introducing students to the specific challenges and rewards of engaging translated works, and also to the cultural effects that translations can have. *Rimbaud's Rainbow*, edited by Peter Bush and Kirsten Malmkjær, contains a wide range of approaches to bringing translation into the classroom, Karen Emmerich's *Translation and the Making of Originals* is fundamental for understanding the text—even the most canonical text—as an unstable object that has undergone, and continues to undergo, extensive processes of mediation.

Of course, one of the simplest ways to foster discussion of the nuances of translation—of a specific work, and generally—is to make sure that students read the translator's note, if there is one, or any interviews with the translator that might be floating about. The translator's notes, for example, that Esther Allen wrote to accompany Rosario Castellanos's *The Book of Lamentations* and Antonio di Benedetto's *Zama* are masterclasses in the form, and Lisa Dillman's note to Yuri Herrera's *Signs Preceding the End of the World* is a lesson unto itself on translation as transcreation and on the plasticity of language.

The narrative representations of translation explored in preceding chapters, however, present a range of issues all their own that can and should be brought into the classroom. The texts discussed need not be the same. For example, "Writing in the Margins" asserted the power of paratexts in the construction (or destruction) of meaning; in response, I have students do close readings of the cover design of different editions across languages and time to analyze the role of framing in the reception of translated works. I ask them to consider what aspects of the book are being emphasized in each context, and to what ideological structures those choices might belong. This exercise has never not generated intense discussions and widespread expressions of surprise at how charged something as apparently innocuous as a cover image or a blurb can be. I also have them discuss the jacket copy and read reviews of the work, to perform a similar analysis of how it is presented (and how translation is discussed, or not, in its coverage).[2] In many courses, I have students write their own reviews of texts they'd like to see included on the syllabus, accounting for existing criticism on the books and also addressing any gaps they were able to find; these reviews are then shared among the group. The goal of this last exercise, beyond having the students share their interests and keep reading after the semester has ended, is to encourage them to see themselves as active participants in a literary community, and understand that the choices they make matter—from where they get their reading recommendations and buy their books, to how they approach the texts that make their way into their hands. This exercise also serves to disrupt the sensation that settles into so many students early on that they are producing work *for* a teacher within a hierarchical relation of authority and approbation.

In a similar vein, the theories and fictions of "Monsters and Parricides" urge us to remember the bright line that connects privately held property and the widely held belief in the subordinate status of translation: both emerge from patrilinear models of ownership. These novels likewise explored the violence of such models, and ultimately proposed horizontal networks of affiliation over and against vertical structures of proprietorship and influence. These issues can be difficult to access when teaching texts that don't address them explicitly, but it is not impossible to do. I make a point of discussing the historical context of each work, regardless of whether it is prominent in the narrative, as well as the material conditions it depicts and those under which it was produced. I encourage the students to ask: Who is laying claim to

---

[2] The same principles hold true for other kinds of cultural objects, particularly those bound to an international marketing apparatus, as films are. In fact, I've done this exercise with different film posters from different countries, and highly recommend the back translation of film titles originally in English to see how they shift in different cultural contexts.

what, both inside and beyond the narrative world presented to us? Then we turn our attention to the book's appearance in English. Why might it have been chosen for translation at the moment that it was? Who translated it, and how is it presented in its new cultural system?

These questions dovetail with those posed in "Writing off the Map," which insists that, while it is possible to carve out spaces of transgression within the neocolonial world system, we are always situated somewhere within it, and there is nothing neutral about the contested territories of our bodies and our worldviews. *Kitchen Table Translation*, edited by Madhu Kaza, is an invaluable resource containing both new translations and critical reflections on precisely the questions outlined above. One of the volume's contributors, Don Mee Choi, wrote an incandescent translator's note to Kim Hyesoon's *All the Garbage of the World, Unite!* that in one page lays bare the violence behind propriety as an editorial criterion, and recently published the manifesto *Translation is a Mode = Translation is an Anti-neocolonial Mode* which centers on the subjective situatedness of the translator and the inherently political nature of translation.[3] A text I turn to again and again, in both the classroom and my own work as a translator, is Gayatri Chakravorty Spivak's "Translating into English," which elucidates the power dynamics among languages and asserts the need for cultural competency over and above linguistic proficiency. Adding another layer of communality to discussions of translation, in this essay Spivak also highlights the responsibility of the teacher in the transmission of a translated work. Looking back on a word choice that flattens the conjoined notion of rights and responsibilities in the Bengali term *hok* into the unidimensional "rights," Spivak reflects, "I have failed in this detail. Translation is as much a problem as it is a solution. I hope the book will be taught by someone who has enough sense of the language to mark this unavoidable failure" (2005: 95).

---

[3] Choi also discusses in this text the representation of translation in Ingmar Bergman's 1963 film, *The Silence*.

What Spivak describes as a failure points, as we saw in "Foreign Correspondence," to an inherent and ultimately positive characteristic of translation, the quality that allows it to defy both fixity and proprietorship. The texts examined in that chapter resisted, with every tool at their disposal, the notion of smooth interlinguistic transfer that subtends the global circulation of cultural goods, and in the process clearly established translation as a creative act. I bring this stance into the classroom through interactive exercises. Just as reading can be a powerful form of transcreation, transcreation can also be a powerful way to read. At the beginning of any course I teach that involves literature in translation, I have students do an exercise that puts them in the role of translators, so they can see first-hand just how many choices go into each word they will see on the page for the rest of the semester. A tried-and-true version of this is having them read either Eliot Weinberger's *Nineteen Ways of Looking at Wang Wei* or Margaret Sayers Peden's "Building a Translation, the Reconstruction Business: Poem 145 of Sor Juana Inés de la Cruz," both of which present a rigorous trot to the poem at hand, followed by an analysis of translations that bridge several centuries and shifting aesthetic tides. Before discussing the translations in any detail, I have students create their own versions with the tools at their disposal, which are more numerous than they first imagine. This presses them to think about things like register, and how to choose between different elements (cadence, structure, rhyme, image) when they realize they can't capture them all. After this, they are not only more invested in the question of translation, they are also able to discuss the choices of other translators in greater depth.

Other creative exercises that foreground translational choice include intra-lingual translations (rendering a horoscope in Shakespearean English, or a passage from a nineteenth-century novel in the contemporary slang of their choice, for example). When working with a group that shares a language in addition to English, I like to present students with a passage in that language and in English and have them talk through which one they think is the translation, and why. This, above all, reveals the preconceptions and normative tendencies we all harbor in one way or another. Finally, it can be illuminating (and amusing) to have students filter a short passage or poem through different languages in Google Translate, stopping off at English between each iteration and capturing the results as the text is increasingly deformed. While this exercise definitely serves as a cautionary tale about translation software, it is also an excellent catalyst for discussing the different levels on which sense is constructed, the importance of contextual knowledge, and the dangers inherent to the promise of having the world at one's fingertips.

These exercises might seem familiar to those who have taught translation, but I believe they would represent an important new paradigm for all students of literature. For any reader of translations, really. By shifting their understanding of texts from a model in which the author is the sole proprietor of the work to one in which the text is shaped by multiple actors from transmission to reception, readers would begin to develop a more flexible and more nuanced understanding of the books in their hands. They would begin to observe their own positionality in the network of relations that is any act of reading; this, ideally, pushes them to engage the translated text in detail while still respecting the distance that separates them from its site of enunciation. To be inquisitive but not acquisitive. Returning to the question of possible futures, then, it is my hope that readers, aligned with the translation narratives here explored, will become attuned to the multiplicity of voices, including their own, that goes into any act of poiesis—which is always an act of teleopoiesis, of creation across and through distance.

Acknowledgments

Every project has an origin story (when not more than one). This book began, somewhat indirectly, with an undergraduate honors thesis gone awry and an offhanded suggestion to try a translation instead. My immense and lasting gratitude to Richard Sieburth for introducing me to the wonders of the practice and theory of translation, and for humoring my youthful hubris when I chose a play written in rhymed verse as my very first project. Eliot Weinberger's patient and precise edits of my work with the poetry of Oliverio Girondo, and the conversations we've continued to this day, have been incredibly formative. Among other things, I will never look at a definite article the same way again.

As this project began to take form as a dissertation on the literary representation of translators, it was indelibly marked by the readings and guidance of Carlos J. Alonso and Graciela Montaldo, who first exposed me to many of the writers studied in these pages, and whose balance of rigor and delight in her objects of study informs my understanding of what scholarship can be. I am also deeply grateful for the insightful feedback of the other members of my committee: Peter Connor, whom I was fortunate enough to assist in his lecture on translation theory and the organization of the Barnard Translation Conference in 2015; Alessandra Russo, who brought an invaluable disciplinary and methodological perspective to this project in its earliest stages; and Jacques Lezra, who has continued to offer his time and expertise with tremendous generosity over the years.

Any words of thanks I could offer Michelle Woods and Brian Baer would fall grievously short. One hopes to work with an editor who knows the field inside and out; who is at once supportive, respectful, and unafraid to give a note. I had not one but two such editors, scholars whose work I admire and whose careful reading of this text was an honor unto itself. My immense thanks to the team at Bloomsbury—especially Haaris Naqvi, Sarah McNamee, and Rachel Moore—and to

Hernán Díaz, who supported this project early on. Lawrence Venuti read Chapter 1 of this book and offered insightful and much appreciated feedback. I am infinitely grateful to Esther Allen for the example she sets as a scholar and translator, but in this context would like to thank her for her incredibly thorough, incredibly illuminating response to this manuscript at an early stage.

I would also like to express my gratitude to the following institutions for their support over the years: the Department of Latin American and Iberian Cultures at Columbia University, where this project began and was supported both materially and intellectually; the Mellon Foundation, which made possible the summer seminar titled "The Problem of Translation" in 2011, which introduced me to new ways of thinking about translation. I am also very grateful to the community of scholars who have invited me to speak over the years on the material presented in this book and who engaged this work vitally at different stages of its development, including Sergio Chejfec, Erin Graff Zivin, Emily Apter, Jacques Lezra, María Julia Rossi, and Douglas Robinson, as well as to the editors and peer reviewers at *Hispanic Review*, who polished and published a version of the chapter "Monsters and Parricides" in 2015. Finally, my immense gratitude to Sarah Lawrence College—for supporting the completion of this volume with leave time and resources for research, for being one of those rare institutions that values translation as a scholarly undertaking, and for being such a vibrant intellectual community.

The people at the College who have enriched my thinking in different ways are too numerous to name, but most certainly include my cherished colleagues in Modern and Classical Languages and Literatures. I am so grateful to library magicians Bobbie Smolow and Geoffrey Danisher, especially as I complete this manuscript in the middle of a pandemic, and to Sayuri Oyama, who generously spent a November afternoon with me unpacking the references to Japanese literature in Mario Bellatin's work. And, of course, to Bella Brodzki, whose exquisite reflection on cultural memory and translation *Can These Bones Live?* (2007) was one of the original inspirations for this project, and whose contributions at various stages of this book have been invaluable. I would also like to recognize the indispensable work of Anamari Gaeta and Caroline Beegan, the student assistants who made it possible for me to juggle classes and writing and translating, and all the students I've had the pleasure of teaching over the course of my five years at Sarah Lawrence. It's a cliché for a reason: I've learned so much from you.

My deepest gratitude stays close to home. To my parents, Heide and Peter, and to my grandparents, for a lifetime of unwavering support. None of this would be possible without you. To the dear friends and interlocutors who have shaped the way I think: Anjuli Fatima Raza Kolb, Valeria Luiselli, Paloma Duong, Julia Sanches, Charlotte Whittle, Mara Faye Lethem, Mieke Chew, Gabriela Jauregui, David Shook, and Mariano Siskind; to the extraordinary members of the Cedilla collective—Sean Gasper Bye, Alex Zucker, Allison Markin Powell, Alta L. Price, Elisabeth Jaquette, Jeffrey Zuckerman, and Jeremy Tiang—you are a constant source of insight and inspiration. And with every fiber of my being to Diego: for always asking the right questions, for your generous critiques, for supporting the completion of this book in ways I never could have imagined, for the ever-expanding universe of thinking with you. Thank you.

Bibliography

Aira, César (1998), "Las dos muñecas" in *La trompeta de mimbre*, Rosario, Argentina: Beatriz Viterbo.
Aira, César (1999), *El congreso de literatura*, Buenos Aires: Tusquets Editores.
Aira, César (2000), *El juego de los mundos*, Buenos Aires: Tusquets Editores.
Aira, César (2003), *La Princesa Primavera*, Mexico: Ediciones Era.
Aira, César (2006), *Parménides*, Barcelona: Mondadori.
Aira, César (2009), "El tiempo y el lugar de la literatura" in *Otra Parte* 19.
Aira, César (2010), *The Literary Conference*, trans. Katherine Silver, New York: New Directions.
Al-Sheikh Hussein, Basel (2012), "The Sapir–Whorf Hypothesis Today" in *Theory and Practice in Language Studies* 2 (3): 642–6.
Alarcón, Norma (1989), "Traddutora, Traditora: A Paradigmatic Figure of Chicana Feminism" in *Cultural Critique* 13: 57–87.
Ali, Tariq (1993), "Literature and Market Realism" in *New Left Review* 199.
Allen, Esther (ed.) (2007), *To Be Translated or Not to Be: PEN/IRL Report on the International Situation of Literary Translators*, New York: PEN American Center.
Allen, Esther (2013), "Footnotes *sans Frontières*: Translation and Textual Scholarship" in Brian Nelson and Brigid Maher (eds.), *Perspectives on Literature and Translation: Creation, Circulation, Reception*, London: Routledge, 210–20.
Allen, Esther (2013), "The Will to Translate: Four Episodes in a Local History of Global Cultural Exchange" in *In Translation: Translators on Their Work and What it Means*, New York: Columbia University Press.
Allen, Esther and Susan Bernofsky (eds.) (2013), *In Translation: Translators on Their Work and What it Means*, New York: Columbia University Press.
Alonso, Carlos J. (1994), "Reading Sarmiento: Once More, with Passion" in *Hispanic Review* 62 (1): 35–52.
Alonso, Carlos J. (2005), "Borges y la teoría" in *MLN* 120 (2): 437–56.
Altamirano, Carlos and Beatriz Sarlo (1983), *Ensayos argentinos: de Sarmiento a la vanguardia*, Buenos Aires: Centro Editor de América Latina.
Altrocchi, Rudolph (1935), *Deceptive Cognates*, Chicago, IL: University of Chicago Press.

Andrade, Oswald de (1991), "Cannibalist Manifesto," trans. Leslie Bary, in *Latin American Literary Review* 19 (38): 38–47.

Aparicio, Frances R. (1991), *Versiones, interpretaciones, creaciones: instancias de la traducción literaria en Hispanoamérica en el siglo veinte*, Gaithersburg, MD: Ediciones Hispamérica.

Appadurai, Arjun (1996), *Modernity at Large: Cultural Dimensions of Globalization*, Minneapolis, MN: University of Minnesota Press.

Apter, Emily (2006), *The Translation Zone: A New Comparative Literature*, Princeton, NJ: Princeton University Press.

Apter, Emily (2013), *Against World Literature: on the Politics of Untranslatability*, New York: Verso.

Arendt, Hannah (1969), "Introduction," trans. Harry Zohn, in Walter Benjamin, *Illuminations*, New York: Random House.

Arrojo, Rosemary (2004a), "Tradução, (in)fidelidade e gênero num conto de Moacyr Scliar" in *Revista brasileira de lingüística aplicada* 4 (1): 27–36.

Arrojo, Rosemary (2004b), "Translation, Transference, and the Attraction to Otherness" in *Diacritics: A Review of Contemporary Criticism* 34 (3–4): 31–53.

Arrojo, Rosemary (2018), *Fictional Translators: Rethinking Translation Through Literature*, London and New York: Routledge.

Austin, Kelly (2003), "Domingo Faustino Sarmiento's Society of Letters in Viajes por Europa, Africa, y América 1845–1847" in *Mester* 32: 103–26.

Austin, Kelly (2008), "'I Have Put All I Possess at the Disposal of the People's Struggle': Pablo Neruda as Collector, Translator, and Poet" in *Comparatist: Journal of the Southern Comparative Literature Association* 32: 40–62.

Averbach, Márgara and Lisa Bradford (eds.) (1997), *Traducción como cultura*, Rosario, Argentina: Beatriz Viterbo Editora.

Baker, Mona (2005), "Narratives in and of Translation" in *SKASE Journal of Translation and Interpretation* 11: 4–13.

Baker, Mona and Gabriela Saldanha (eds.) (2009), *Routledge Encyclopedia of Translation Studies*, London: Routledge.

Balderston, Daniel (2003), "Sexuality and Revolution: On the Footnotes to El beso de la mujer araña," in Matthew C. Gutmann (ed.), *Changing Men and Masculinities in Latin America*, Durham, NC: Duke University Press.

Balderston, Daniel and Marcy Schwartz (eds.) (2002), *Voice-Overs: Translation and Latin American Literature*, Albany, NY: State University of New York Press.

Barnett, Ian (2004), "The Translator as Hero" at: https://www.biblit.it/wp-content/uploads/2014/08/translator_hero.pdf (last accessed May 19, 2020).

Barney, Stephen A. (ed.) (1991), *Annotation and Its Texts*, New York: Oxford University Press.

Bassnett, Susan (1992), "Writing in No Man's Land: Questions of Gender and Translation" in *Ilha do Desterro* 28 (2): 63–73.

Bassnett, Susan and Harish Trivedi (eds.) (1999), *Post-colonial Translation: Theory and Practice*, London and New York: Routledge.

Bassnett, Susan (2002), *Translation Studies*, London and New York: Routledge.

Battistón, Dora (2001), "Borges y la traducción de las últimas páginas del Ulysses de Joyce" in *Anclajes: revista del Instituto de Análisis Semiótico del Discurso* 5 (5): 55–70.

Bellatin, Mario (2000), *El jardín de la señora Murakami: Oto No-Murakami Monogatari*, Mexico: Tusquets Editores.

Bellatin, Mario (2001), *Shiki Nagaoka: una nariz de ficción*, Buenos Aires: Editorial Sudamericana.

Bellatin, Mario (2002), *Jacobo el mutante*, Mexico: Alfaguara.

Bellatin, Mario (2003), *Escritores duplicados: narradores mexicanos en París*, Paris: Landucci Editores.

Bellatin, Mario (2006a), "Lo raro es ser un escritor raro" in *Pájaro transparente*, Buenos Aires: Mansalva, 107–24.

Bellatin, Mario (2006b), *Perros heroes*, Lima: Grupo Editorial Matalamanga.

Bellatin, Mario (2008), "Kawabata: el abrazo del abismo" at *ADN*: https://www.lanacion.com.ar/cultura/kawabata-el-abrazo-del-abismo-nid1002472 (last accessed October 31, 2019).

Bellatin, Mario (2012), *Shiki Nagaoka: A Nose for Fiction*, trans. David Shook, Los Angeles, CA: Phoneme Media.

Bellatin, Mario (2015a), *Jacob the Mutant*, trans. Jacob Steinberg, Los Angeles, CA: Phoneme Media.

Bellatin, Mario (2015b), "Writing Lessons for the Blind and Deaf," trans. David Shook, in *Buenos Aires Review* at: http://www.buenosairesreview.org/2015/05/writing-lessons/ (last accessed July 25, 2020).

Bellatin, Mario (2016), "The Writer's Block: A Video Q&A with Mario Bellatin" at *City of Asylum*: https://www.youtube.com/watch?time_continue=256&v=ewDcDLD_Hyg (last accessed October 13, 2019).

Bellatin, Mario (2020), *Mrs. Murakami's Garden*, trans. Heather Cleary, Dallas, TX: Deep Vellum.

Bellatin, Mario and Graciela Iturbide (2008), *El baño de Frida Kahlo*, Mexico: Galería López Quiroga.

Bellos, David (2011), *Is That a Fish in Your Ear? Translation and the Meaning of Everything*, New York: Faber and Faber.

Benesdra, Salvador (1998), *El traductor*, Buenos Aires: Ediciones de la Flor.

Benjamin, Walter (2005), in Rodney Livingstone et al. (eds.), *Selected Writings*, Cambridge, MA: Harvard University Press.

Bermann, Sandra and Michael Wood (eds.) (2005), *Nation, Language, and the Ethics of Translation*, Princeton, NJ: Princeton University Press.

Bhabha, Homi K. (2004), *The Location of Culture*, London: Routledge.

Block de Behar, Lisa (2003), *Borges: The Passion of an Endless Quotation*, Albany, NY: SUNY Press.

Bloom, Harold (1973), *The Anxiety of Influence*, New York: Oxford University Press.

Boon, Marcus (2010), *In Praise of Copying*, Cambridge, MA: Harvard University Press.

Borges, Jorge Luis (1925), *Inquisiciones*, Buenos Aires: Editorial Proa.

Borges, Jorge Luis (1996 [1936]), "Los traductores de las 1001 noches," in *Obras Completas I*, Barcelona: Emecé Editores, 397–413.

Borges, Jorge Luis (1997a [1932]), *Discusión*, Madrid: Alianza Editorial.

Borges, Jorge Luis (1997b [1952]), *Otras Inquisiciones*, Madrid: Alianza Editorial.

Borges, Jorge Luis (1999), *Collected Fictions*, trans. Andrew Hurley, New York: Penguin Books.

Borges, Jorge Luis (2000), *Selected Non-Fictions*, trans. Eliot Weinberger, Esther Allen, and Susanne Jill Levine, New York: Penguin Books.

Borges, Jorge Luis (2011), *Cuentos completos*, Mexico: Lumen Editorial.

Bourdieu, Pierre (1991), in John B. Thompson (ed.), *Language and Symbolic Power*, Cambridge, MA: Harvard University Press.

Bourdieu, Pierre (1993), in Randal Johnson (ed.), *The Field of Cultural Production: Essays on Art and Literature*, New York: Columbia University Press.

Bradford, Lisa (1997), "Introducción" in Márgara Averbach and Lisa Bradford (eds.), *Traducción como cultura*, Rosario, Argentina: Beatriz Viterbo Editora, 13–24.

Brodzki, Bella (2007), *Can These Bones Live? Translation, Survival, and Cultural Memory*, Stanford, CA: Stanford University Press.

Buarque, Chico (2003), *Budapeste: romance*, São Paulo: Companhia das Letras.

Buarque, Chico (2004), *Budapest*, trans. Alison Entrekin, New York: Grove Press.

Bucher, Matt (2016), "The Greatest Mexican Experimental Sufi Novelist You've Never Heard Of" at *Electric Literature*: https://electricliterature.com/the-greatest-mexican-experimental-sufi-novelist-youve-never-heard-of/ (last accessed October 13, 2019).

Bush, Peter and Kirsten Malmkjær (eds.) (1998), *Rimbaud's Rainbow: Literary Translation in Higher Education*, Amsterdam: John Benjamins Publishing Company.

Campos, Augusto de (1995), "Um diálogo quase visceral com a tradução" at *Humboldt: uma publicação do Goethe Institut*: http://www.goethe.de/wis/bib/prj/hmb/the/das/pt3289334.htm (last accessed June 9, 2020).

Campos, Haroldo de (1981), "Da razão antropofágica. A Europa sob o signo da devoração" in *Colóquio/Letras* 62: 10–25.

Campos, Haroldo de (1986), "The Rule of Anthropophagy: Europe under the Sign of Devoration," trans. María Tai Wolff, in *Latin American Literary Review* 14 (27): 42–60.

Campos, Haroldo de (1992), *Metalinguagem & outras metas: ensaios de teoria e crítica literária*, São Paulo: Editora Perspectiva.

Campos, Haroldo de (2007), in Antonio Sergio Bessa and Odile Cisneros (eds.), *Novas: Selected Writings*, Evanston, IL: Northwestern University Press.

Capano, Daniel A. (2006), "Borges y los orangutanes eternos de Luis F Verissimo, parodia del thriller culto" in *Letras de hoje* 41 (4): 93–100.

Carilla, Emilio (1989), "Los epígrafes y la elaboración del Facundo" in *Boletín de la Academia Argentina de Letras* 54 (211–12): 131–69.

Carilla, Emilio (1990), "Borges, Alfonso Reyes … y, de nuevo, 'Pierre Menard'" in *Alba de América* 8 (14–15): 203–10.

Casanova, Pascale (2004), *The World Republic of Letters*, trans. M. B. Debevoise, Cambridge, MA: Harvard University Press.

Cassin, Barbara, et al. (eds.) (2014), *Dictionary of Untranslatables: A Philosophical Lexicon*, Princeton, NJ: Princeton University Press.

Cassin, Barbara (2016), "Translation as Paradigm for Human Sciences" in *The Journal of Speculative Philosophy* 30 (3): 242–66.

Catford, J. C. (1965), *A Linguistic Theory of Translation: An Essay in Applied Linguistics*, London: Oxford University Press.

Catelli, Nora and Marietta Gargatagli (eds.) (1998), *El tabaco que fumaba Plinio: escenas de la traducción en España y América*, Barcelona: Del Serbal.

Chabod, Cecilia (2008), "El ejercicio de la traducción y la elusiva frontera entre mostrarse y desaparecer: A propósito de 'nota al pie' de Rodolfo Walsh" in *Páginas de Guarda* 6: 97–110.

Chacón Beltrán, Rubén (2006), "Towards a Typological Classification of False Friends (Spanish–English)" in *Revista española de lingüística aplicada* 19: 29–39.

Chamberlain, Lori (1988), "Gender and the Metaphorics of Translation," *Signs* 13 (3): 454–72.

Choi, Don Mee (2011), "Translator's Note" in Kim Hyesoon, *All the Garbage of the World, Unite!*, Notre Dame, IL: Action Books.

Choi, Don Mee (2020), *Translation is a Mode = Translation is an Antineocolonial Mode*, New York: Ugly Duckling Presse.

Cleary, Heather (2013), "Mario Bellatin's *Shiki Nagaoka: A Nose for Fiction*" at *Words Without Borders*: https://www.wordswithoutborders.org/book-review/mario-bellatins-shiki-nagaoka-a-nose-for-fiction (last accessed October 13, 2019).

Cleary, Heather (2015), "Mario Bellatin's *Jacob the Mutant*" at *Music and Literature*: http://www.musicandliterature.org/reviews/2015/4/20/mario-bellatins-jacob-the-mutant (last accessed October 13, 2019).

Cohen, Marcelo (1995), *El testamento de O'Jaral*, Madrid: A&M Muchnik.

Colás, Santiago (1994), *Postmodernity in Latin America: The Argentine Paradigm*, Durham, NC: Duke University Press.

Cortázar, Julio (1998), "Letter to a Young Lady in Paris," trans. Paul Blackburn, in *Bestiary: Selected Stories*, London: Harvill Press, 8–14.

Cortázar, Julio (2011), "Carta a una señorita en París" in *Bestiario*, Buenos Aires: Aguilar, Altea, Taurus, Alfaguara.

Cosgrove, Peter (1991), "Undermining the Text: Edward Gibbon, Alexander Pope, and the Anti-Authenticating Footnote" in Stephen A. Barney (ed.), *Annotation and Its Texts*, New York: Oxford University Press, 130–51.

Cronin, Michael (2003), *Translation and Globalization*, London: Routledge.

Curran, Beverly (2007), "The Embedded Translator: A Coming Out Story" in Myriam Salama-Carr (ed.), *Translating and Interpreting Conflict*, Amsterdam: Rodopi, 233–52.

Damrosch, David (2003), *What is World Literature?*, Princeton, NJ: Princeton University Press.

Daniel, Sharon (2007), "The Database: An Aesthetics of Dignity" in Victoria Vesna (ed.), *Database Aesthetics: Art in the Age of Information Overflow*, Minneapolis, MN: University of Minnesota Press: 142–82.

De Man, Paul (1986), *The Resistance to Theory*, Minneapolis, MN: University of Minnesota Press.

Delabastita, Dirk and Rainier Grutman (2005), "Introduction: Fictional representations of multilingualism and translation" in *Linguistica Antverpiensia* 4: 11–34.

Deleuze, Gilles, and Félix Guattari (1986), *Kafka: Toward a Minor Literature*, trans. Dana Polen, Minneapolis, MN: University of Minnesota Press.

Deleuze, Gilles and Félix Guattari (1987), *A Thousand Plateaus: Capitalism and Schizophrenia*, trans. Brian Massumi, Minneapolis, MN: University of Minnesota Press.

Delisle, Jean and Judith Woodsworth (eds.) (1995), *Translators Through History*, Amsterdam: John Benjamins Publishing Company.

Derrida, Jacques (1985a), "Des Tours de Babel," trans. Joseph F. Graham, in Joseph F. Graham (ed.), *Difference in Translation*, Ithaca, NY: Cornell University Press, 165–208.

Derrida, Jacques (1985b), in Christie, McDonald (ed.), *The Ear of the Other: Otobiography, Transference, Translation*, New York: Schocken Books.

Derrida, Jacques (1991), "This is not an Oral Footnote" in Stephen A. Barney (ed.), *Annotation and its Texts*, New York: Oxford University Press, 192–206.

Derrida, Jacques (1996), *Le monolinguisme de l'autre: ou la prothèse d'origine*, Paris: Galilée.

Derrida, Jacques (1998), *Monolingualism of the Other, or, The Prosthesis of Origin*, trans. Patrick Mensah, Stanford, CA: Stanford University Press.

Derrida, Jacques (2005), *The Politics of Friendship*, trans. George Collins, New York: Verso.

Díaz, Hernán (2012), *Borges, Between History and Eternity*, New York: Bloomsbury.

Driver, Alice (2013), "Dark Humor and the Horror of Postmodernity" in *Voices of Mexico* 96: 105–8.

Duarte, Pablo (2009), "Elogio de la inventiva: entrevista con César Aira" at *Letras libres*: https://www.letraslibres.com/mexico-espana/elogio-la-inventiva-entrevista-cesar-aira (last accessed April 16, 2020).

Eco, Umberto (2000), *Experiences in Translation*, Toronto: University of Toronto Press.

Emmerich, Karen (2017), *Literary Translation and the Making of Originals*, New York: Bloomsbury.

Emmerich, Michael (2013), "Beyond, Between: Translation, Ghosts, Metaphors" in Esther Allen and Susan Bernofsky (eds.), *In Translation:*

Translators on their Work and What it Means, New York: Columbia University Press, 44–57.

Epplin, Craig (2014), *Late Book Culture in Argentina*, New York: Bloomsbury.

Even-Zohar, Itamar (1979), "Polysystem Theory" in *Poetics Today: Special Issue: Literature, Interpretation, Communication* 1 (1/2): 287–310.

Feierstein, Liliana Ruth (2008), "N. de la T.: los pies del texto" in Liliana Ruth Feierstein and Vera Elisabeth Gerling (eds.), *Traducción y poder: sobre marginados, infieles, hermeneutas y exiliados*, Madrid: Iberoamericana, 17–34.

Fishburn, Evelyn (2002), "A Footnote to Borges Studies: A Study of the Footnotes" in *Institute of Latin American Studies Occasional Papers* 26: 1–23.

Foucault, Michel (1984), in Paul Rabinow (ed.), *The Foucault Reader*, New York: Pantheon Books.

Garrels, Elizabeth (1993), "Traducir a América: Sarmiento y el proyecto de una literatura nacional" in *Revista de Crítica Literaria Latinoamericana* 19 (38): 269–78.

Gaspar, Martín (2011), "The new task of the translator in Latin American fiction: the case of Alan Pauls' *The Past*" in *Latin American Literary Review* 78: 73–94.

Gaspar, Martín (2014), *La condición traductora: sobre los nuevos protagonistas de la literatura latinoamericana*, Rosario: Beatriz Viterbo Editora.

Genette, Gerard (1977), *Paratexts: Thresholds of Interpretation*, trans. Jane E. Lewin, New York: Cambridge University Press.

Gentzler, Edwin (2007), *Translation and Identity in the Americas*, New York: Routledge.

Geraghty, Niall H. D. (2018), *The Polyphonic Machine: Capitalism, Political Violence, and Resistance in Contemporary Argentine Literature*, Pittsburgh, PA: University of Pittsburg Press.

Girondo, Oliverio (1999), in Raúl Antelo (ed.), *Obras completas*, Madrid: Galaxia Gutenberg.

Glantz, Margo (1992), "Las hijas de la Malinche" in *debate feminista* 6: 161–79.

Glantz, Margo (1994), "La Malinche: la lengua en la mano" in *debate feminista* 10: 167–82.

Godayol, Pilar (2012), "Malintzin/La Malinche/Doña Marina: Re-reading the myth of the treacherous translator" in *Journal of Iberian and Latin American Studies* 18 (1): 61–76.

Godayol, Pilar (2013), "Metaphors, women and translation: From *les belles infidèles* to *la frontera*" in *Gender and Language* 7 (1): 97–116.

Gómez López-Quiñones, Antonio (2001), "En los márgenes de Borges: Las notas a pie de página en 'Deutsches requiem' y 'Pierre Menard'" in *Variaciones Borges* 12: 139–65.

Grafton, Anthony (1994), "The Footnote from De Thou to Ranke" in *History and Theory* 33 (4): 53–76.

Grafton, Anthony (1997), "Birth of the Footnote" in *Lingua Franca: The Review of Academic Life* 7 (9): 59–66.

Grafton, Anthony (1999), *The Footnote: A Curious History*, Cambridge, MA: Harvard University Press.

Graham, Joseph F. (ed.) (1985), *Difference in Translation*, Ithaca, NY: Cornell University Press.

Granger, Sylviane and Helen Swallow (1988), "False Friends: A Kaleidoscope of Translation Difficulties" in *Le Langage et l'Homme* 23 (2): 108–20.

Grossman, Edith (2010), *Why Translation Matters*, New Haven, CT: Yale University Press.

Guzmán, Claudia Aburto (2010), "La traducción como acto ético-moral en los territorios fronterizos: o por qué la voz lírica de Demetria Martínez" in *Revista Hispánica Moderna* 63 (1): 1–17.

Guzmán, María Costanza (2006), "The Spectrum of Translation in Julio Cortázar's 'Letter to a Young Lady in Paris'" in *Ikala: revista de lenguaje y cultura* 11 (17): 75–86.

Haberly, David T. (2005), "Francis Bond Head and Domingo Sarmiento: A Note on the Sources of *Facundo*" in *MLN* 120 (2): 287–93.

Halperín Donghi, Tulio, Francine Masiello, Iván Jaksic, and Gwen Kirkpatrick (eds.) (1994), *Sarmiento, Author of a Nation*, Berkeley, CA: University of California Press.

Hayles, Katherine (2008), *Electronic Literature: New Horizons for the Literary*, Notre Dame, IN: University of Notre Dame Press.

Hayot, Eric (2005), "I/O: A Comparative Literature in a Digital Age" in *Comparative Literature* 57 (3): 219–26.

Hermans, Theo (ed.) (1985), *The Manipulation of Literature: Studies in Literary Translation*, New York: St. Martin's Press.

Hermans, Theo (1996), "Translation's Other," a lecture at University College London, available at: https://core.ac.uk/download/pdf/1668908.pdf (last accessed June 10, 2020).

Hermosillo Sánchez, Alejandro (2011), "Mario Bellatin: complaciente y cruel" in *El coloquio de los perros* at: https://elcoloquiodelosperros.weebly.com/uploads/2/5/3/3/25330873/el-coloquio-de-los-perros-mb.pdf (last accessed June 10, 2020).

Hind, Emily (2002), "Novel Globalization: Mario Bellatín's *El jardín de la señora Murakami*" in *Hispanic Journal* 23 (1): 21–34.

Humboldt, Wilhelm von (1992), "Introduction to His Translation of *Agamemnon*," trans. Sharon Sloan, in Ranier Schulte and John Biguenet (eds.), *Theories of Translation*, Chicago, IL: University of Chicago Press, 55–9.

Hutchins, W. John (ed.) (2000), *Early Years in Machine Translation: Memoirs and Biographies of Pioneers*, Amsterdam: John Benjamins Publishing Company.

Jacobs, Carol (1975), "The Monstrosity of Translation" in *MLN* 90 (6): 755–66.

Jacobs, Carol (1999), *In the Language of Walter Benjamin*, Baltimore, MD: Johns Hopkins University Press.

Jakobson, Roman (1992), "On Linguistic Aspects of Translation" in Ranier Schulte and John Biguenet (eds.), *Theories of Translation*, Chicago, IL: University of Chicago Press, 144–51.

Jitrik, Noé (1968), *Muerte y resurrección de Facundo*, Buenos Aires: Centro Editor de América Latina.

Johnson, Barbara (1985), "Taking Fidelity Philosophically" in Joseph F. Graham (ed.), *Difference in Translation*, Ithaca, NY: Cornell University Press, 142–8.

Kaindl, Klaus and Karlheinz Spitzl (eds.) (2014), *Transfiction: Research into the Realities of Translation Fiction*, Amsterdam: John Benjamins Publishing Company.

Kaindl, Klaus, Nitsa Ben-Ari, Patricia Godbout, and Shaul Levin (eds.) (2016), *Beyond Transfiction: Translators and their Authors*, a special issue of *Translation and Interpreting Studies*, Amsterdam: John Benjamins Publishing Company.

Katchadjian, Pablo (2007), *El Martín Fierro ordenado alfabéticamente*, Buenos Aires: Imprenta Argentina de Poesía.

Katchadjian, Pablo (2010), *Qué hacer*, Buenos Aires: Bajo la Luna.

Katra, William H. (1996), *The Argentine Generation of 1837: Echeverría, Alberdi, Sarmiento, Mitre*, Madison, NJ: Fairleigh Dickinson University Press.

Kaza, Madhu (ed.) (2017), *Kitchen Table Translation*, Pittsburgh, PA: Blue Sketch Press.

Kittler, Friedrich A. (1999), *Gramophone, Film, Typewriter*, trans. Geoffrey Winthrop-Young and Michael Wutz, Stanford, CA: Stanford University Press.

Klotzko, Arlene (ed.) (2001), *The Cloning Sourcebook*, New York: Oxford University Press.

Koessler, Maxime (1964), *Les faux amis; ou, Les pièges du vocabulaire anglais (conseils aux traducteurs)*, Paris: Vuibert.

Kolata, Gina (2001), "Researchers Find Big Risk of Defect in Cloning Animals" in *The New York Times*, at: https://www.nytimes.com/2001/03/25/world/researchers-find-big-risk-of-defect-in-cloning-animals.html (last accessed April 13, 2020).

Kripper, Denise (2017), "Los agentes de la traducción: las ficciones del traductor como relatos de mercado" in *Mutatis Mutandis* 10 (2): 174–94.

Kristal, Efraín (2002), *Invisible Work: Borges and Translation*, Nashville, TN: Vanderbilt University Press.

Laddaga, Reinaldo (2007), *Espectáculos de realidad: ensayo sobre la narrativa latinoamericana de las últimas dos décadas*, Rosario: Beatriz Viterbo Editora.

Landow, George P. (2006), *Hypertext 3.0: Critical Theory and New Media in an Era of Globalization*, Baltimore, MD: Johns Hopkins University Press.

Laraway, David (2000), "Generations: Borges and His Progeny" in *Latin American Literary Review* 28 (56): 27–42.

Lefevere, André (1992), *Translation, Rewriting, and the Manipulation of Literary Fame*, London and New York: Routledge.

Lefevre, Andre (ed.) (1992), *Translation – History – Culture: A Sourcebook*, London: Routledge.

Lennon, Brian (2010), *In Babel's Shadow: Multilingual Literatures, Monolingual States*, Minneapolis, MN: University of Minnesota Press.

Leone, Leah (2008), "La novela cautiva: Borges y la traducción de Orlando" in *Variaciones Borges* 25: 223–36.

Lewkowicz, Javier (2015), "Post-neoliberalism: Lessons from South America" at https://www.opendemocracy.net/en/opendemocracyuk/postneoliberalism-lessons-from-south-america/ (last accessed June 19, 2020).

Lezra, Jacques (2008), "The Indecisive Muse: Ethics in Translation and the Idea of History" in *Comparative Literature* 60 (4): 301–30.

Lezra, Jacques (2012), "Translation" in *Political Concepts* at: http://www.politicalconcepts.org/translation-jacques-lezra/ (last accessed June 10, 2020).

Lezra, Jacques (2017), *Untranslating Machines: A Genealogy for the Ends of Global Thought*, London and New York: Rowman & Littlefield International.

Link, Daniel (2008), "La Nación no gana para sustos" on the blog *Linkillo*, at: http://linkillo.blogspot.com/2008/04/la-nacin-no-gana-para-sustos.html (last accessed November 1, 2019).

Liu, Lydia H. (ed.) (1999), *Tokens of Exchange: The Problem of Translation in Global Circulations*, Durham, NC: Duke University Press.

Lopez, Adam (2008), "Statistical machine translation" in *ACM Computing Survey* 40 (3): 1–49.

López-Calvo, Ignacio (2013), *The Affinity of the Eye: Writing Nikkei in Peru*, Tucson, AZ: University of Arizona Press.

Luiselli, Valeria (2011), *Los ingrávidos*, Mexico: Sexto Piso.

Luiselli, Valeria (2014), *Faces in the Crowd*, trans. Christina MacSweeney, Minneapolis, MN: Coffee House Press.

Luiselli, Valeria (2015), "Translation Spaces: Mexico City in the International Modernist Circuit," Doctoral dissertation, New York: Columbia University.

Macadam, Alfred (1975), "Translation as Metaphor: Three Versions of Borges" in *MLN* 90 (6): 747–54.

Mairal, Pedro (2005), *El año del desierto*, Buenos Aires: Interzona.

Manovich, Lev (2007), "Database as Symbolic Form," in Victoria Vesna (ed.), *Database Aesthetics: Art in the Age of Information Overflow*, Minneapolis, MN: University of Minnesota Press, 39–60.

Masiello, Francine (2001), *The Art of Transition: Latin American Culture and Neoliberal Crisis*, Durham, NC: Duke University Press.

Mayali, Laurent (1991), "For a Political Economy of Annotation" in Stephen A. Barney (ed.), *Annotation and its Texts*, New York: Oxford University Press, 185–91.

McLuhan, Marshall (1962), *The Gutenberg Galaxy: The Making of Typographic Man*, Toronto: University of Toronto Press.

Miller, Stephen Paul and Daniel Morris (eds.) (2009), *Radical Poetics and Secular Jewish Culture*, Tuscaloosa, AL: University of Alabama Press.

Milton, John and Paul F. Bandia (eds.) (2009), *Agents of Translation*, Amsterdam: John Benjamins Publishing Company.

Mochkofsky, Graciela (2015), "Mexico's Literary Prankster Goes to War with his Publisher" in *The New Yorker*, at: https://www.newyorker.com/books/page-turner/mexicos-literary-prankster-goes-to-war-with-his-publisher (last accessed October 13, 2019).

Molloy, Sylvia (1988), "Sarmiento, lector de sí mismo en *Recuerdos de provincia*" in *Revista Iberoamericana* 54 (143): 407–18.

Montaldo, Graciela (1998), "Borges, Aira y la literatura para multitudes" at *Reunión del Centro de Estudios de Teoría y Crítica Literaria en Rosario, Argentina*: http://www.celarg.org/int/arch_publi/montaldob6.pdf.

Montaldo, Graciela (2006), "La expulsión de la república, la deserción del mundo" in Ignacio Sánchez Prado (ed.), *América Latina en la "literatura mundial,"* Pittsburgh, PA: University of Pittsburgh Press, 255–70.

Montezanti, Miguel Angel (1997), "'Traducción y pluralismo cultural'" in Márgara Averbach and Lisa Bradford (eds.), *Traducción como cultura*, Rosario, Argentina: Beatriz Viterbo Editora, 155–66.

Moretti, Franco (2000), "Conjectures on World Literature" in *New Left Review* 1: 54–67.

Mounin, Georges (1955), *Les Belles infidèles*, Paris: Cahiers du Sud.

Mounin, Georges (1971), *Los problemas teóricos de la traducción*, Madrid: Editorial Gredos.

Nelkin, Dorothy and M. Susan Lindee (2001), "Cloning in the Popular Imagination" in Arlene Klotzko (ed.), *The Cloning Sourcebook*, New York: Oxford University Press, 83–93.

Neuman, Andrés (2013), *Traveler of the Century*, trans. Nick Caistor and Lorenza García, New York: Farrar, Straus & Giroux.

Nida, Eugene (2002), *Contexts in Translating*, Amsterdam: John Benjamins Publishing Company.

Niranjana, Tejaswini (1992) *Siting Translation: History, Post-structuralism, and the Colonial Context*, Berkeley, CA: University of California Press.

Orloff, Ulrike (2005), "Who Wrote This Text and Who Cares?" in José Santaemilia (ed.), *Gender, Sex and Translation: The Manipulation of Identities*, Manchester: St. Jerome.

Osset, Miquel (1998), "La enfermedad del mundo: Entrevista a Alan Pauls" in *Quimera: Revista de Literatura* 167: 34–8.

Pagano, Adriana (2002), "Translation as Testimony: On Official Histories and Subversive Pedagogies in Cortázar" in Maria Tymoczko and Edwin Gentzler (eds.), *Translation and Power*, Amherst, MA: University of Massachusetts Press.

Pagni, Andrea, Gertrudis Payàs, and Patricia Willson (eds.) (2011), *Traductores y traducciones en la historia cultural de América Latina*, Mexico: UNAM.

Pajares Tosca, Susana (2004), *Literatura digital: el paradigma hypertextual*, Cáceres: Universidad de Extremadura.

Palaversich, Diana (2003), "Apuntes para una lectura de Mario Bellatin" in *Chasqui: Revista de Literatura Latinoamericana* 32 (1): 25–38.

Palumbo-Liu, David, Bruce W. Robbins, and Nirvana Tanoukhi (eds.) (2011), *Immanuel Wallerstein and the Problem of the World: System, Scale, Culture*, Durham, NC: Duke University Press.

Pape, María (2015), "El pasaje como *modus operandi*: perspectivas simultáneas y recíprocamente excluyentes en *Los ingrávidos* de Valeria Luiselli" in *Revista chilena de literatura* 90: 171–95.

Pauls, Alan (2003), *El pasado*, Barcelona: Editorial Anagrama.

Pauls, Alan (2005), "El problema Bellatin" in *El coloquio de los perros* at: https://elcoloquiodelosperros.weebly.com/uploads/2/5/3/3/25330873/el-coloquio-de-los-perros-mb.pdf (last accessed June 10, 2020).

Pauls, Alan (2007), *The Past*, trans. Nick Caistor, London: Harvill Secker.

Pauls, Alan (2010), *Historia del pelo*, Barcelona: Editorial Anagrama.

Paz, Octavio (1971), *Traducción: literatura y literalidad*, Barcelona: Tusquets Editores.

Paz, Octavio (1974), *Versiones y diversiones*, Mexico: J. Mortiz.

Paz, Octavio (1992), "Translation: Literature and Letters," trans. Irene del Corral, in John Biguenet and Ranier Schulte (eds.), *Theories of Translation*, Chicago, IL: University of Chicago Press, 152–62.

Pellicer, Jaime O. (1990), *El Facundo: significante y significado*, Buenos Aires: Editorial Trilce.

Piglia, Ricardo (1975), *Nombre falso*, Mexico: Siglo Veintiuno Editores.

Piglia, Ricardo (1990), *Crítica y ficción*, Buenos Aires: Siglo Veinte.

Piglia, Ricardo (1994), "Sarmiento the Writer" in Tulio Halperín Donghi, et al. (eds.), *Sarmiento, Author of a Nation*, Berkeley, CA: University of California Press, 127–44.

Piglia, Ricardo (2001), *La ciudad ausente*, Barcelona: Editorial Anagrama.

Piglia, Ricardo (2001), *Respiración artificial*, Barcelona: Editorial Anagrama.

Piper, Andrew (2012), *Book Was There: Reading in Electronic Times*, Chicago, IL: University of Chicago Press.

Pires Vieira, Else Ribeiro (1998), "New Registers for Translation in Latin America" in Peter Bush and Kirsten Malmkjaer (eds.), *Rimbaud's Rainbow:*

Literary Translation in Higher Education, Amsterdam: John Benjamins Publishing Company, 171–95.

Pires Vieira, Else Ribeiro (1999), "Liberating Calibans: readings of *Antropofagia* and Haroldo de Campos' poetics of transcreation" in Susan Bassnett and Harish Trivedi (eds.), *Post-colonial Translation: Theory and Practice*, London: Routledge, 95–113.

Pizer, John (2000), "Goethe's 'World Literature' Paradigm and Contemporary Cultural Globalization" in *Comparative Literature* 52 (3): 213–27.

Ponce, Néstor (1998), *El intérprete*. Rosario, Argentina: Beatriz Viterbo Editora.

Pratt, Mary Louise (2002), "The Traffic in Meaning: Translation, Contagion, Infiltration" in *Profession*, 25–36.

Pratt, Mary Louise, et al. (2009), "Translation Studies Forum: Cultural Translation" in *Translation Studies* 3 (1): 94–110.

Prendergast, Christopher (2001), "Negotiating World Literature" in *New Left Review* 8: 100–21.

Puig, Manuel (1976), *El beso de la mujer araña*, Barcelona: Seix Barral.

Pym, Anthony (1995), "Schleiermacher and the Problem of Blendlinge" in *Translation and Literature* 4 (1): 5–30.

Pym, Anthony (2004), *The Moving Text: Localization, Translation, and Distribution*, Amsterdam: John Benjamins Publishing Company.

Reber, Dierdra (2007), "Cure for the Capitalist Headache: Affect and Fantastic Consumption in César Aira's Argentine 'Baghdad'" in *MLN* 122 (2): 371–99.

Rénique, Gerardo (2005), "Introduction" in *Latin America Today: The Revolt Against Neoliberalism*, 19 (3): 1–11.

Rivera Garza, Cristina (2012), *El mal de la taiga*, Barcelona: Tusquets Editores.

Rivera Garza, Cristina (2018), *The Taiga Syndrome*, trans. Suzanne Jill Levine and Aviva Kana, St. Louis, MO: Dorothy, A Publishing Project.

Rivera Garza, Cristina (2019), "You Will Find Me Upriver: Dissent and Translation," an interview with Maddie King for *Bloom*, January 22, available at: https://bloom-site.com/2019/01/22/you-will-find-me-upriver-dissent-and-translation-qa-w-cristina-rivera-garza/ (last accessed April 30, 2020).

Robinson, Douglas (1996), *Translation & Taboo*, DeKalb, IL: Northern Illinois University Press.

Robinson, Douglas (1997), *What is Translation? Centrifugal Theories, Critical Interventions*, Kent, OH: Kent State University Press.

Roca Varela, María Luisa (2011), "Teaching and Learning 'False Friends': A Review of Some Useful Resources," *Encuentro* 20: 80–7.

Rohter, Larry (2009), "A Mischievous Novelist with an Eye and and Ear for the Unusual," *The New York Times*, August 9, available at: https://www.nytimes.com/2009/08/10/books/10bellatin.html (last accessed October 13, 2019).

Romano-Sued, Susana (1997), "Borges y la ficción como crítica: ficción, abismo y metatextualidad" in Márgara Averbach and Lisa Bradford (eds.), *Traducción como cultura*, Rosario, Argentina: Beatriz Viterbo Editora, 167–86.

Ronell, Avital (2008), in Diane Davis (ed.), *The ÜberReader: Selected Works of Avital Ronell*, Urbana, IL: University of Illinois Press.

Rosman, Silvia N. (1998), "Of Travelers, Foreigners and Nomads: The Nation in Translation," *Latin American Literary Review* 26 (51): 17–29.

Rutherford, Jonathan (1990), "The Third Space: Interview with Homi Bhabha," *Identity: Community, Culture, Difference*, London: Lawrence and Wishart, 207–21.

Saer, Juan José (1969), *Cicatrices*, Buenos Aires: Editorial Sudamericana.

Saer, Juan José (1988), *Glosa*, Barcelona: Destino.

Saer, Juan José (2011), *Scars*, trans. Steve Dolph, Rochester, NY: Open Letter Books.

Safranchik, Graciela (1995), *El cangrejo*, Buenos Aires: Bajo la Luna.

Sagastume, Jorge and Miguel Martínez-Saenz (2005), "Desmantelamiento y reconstrucción textual: Borges, 'Pierre Menard, autor del Quijote' y la traducción" in *Bulletin of Spanish Studies* 82 (6): 815–29.

Salama-Carr, Myriam (ed.) (2007), *Translating and Interpreting Conflict*, Amsterdam: Rodopi.

Salas-Elorza, Jesús (2004), "Shiki Nagaoka: Una nariz de ficción. La novela como hipertexto" in *Revista de Literatura Mexicana Contemporánea* 10 (24): 65–72.

Sánchez Prado, Ignacio (ed.) (2006), *América Latina en la "literatura mundial,"* Pittsburgh, PA: Pittsburgh University Press.

Santiago, Silviano (2001), "The Space In-between," trans. Ana Lúcia Gazzola and Gareth Williams, in *The Space In-between: Essays on Latin American Culture*, Durham, NC: Duke University Press.

Santis, Pablo de (1998), *La traducción*, Buenos Aires: Planeta.

Sarlo, Beatriz (1988), *Una modernidad periférica: Buenos Aires, 1920 y 1930*, Buenos Aires: Ediciones Nueva Visión.

Sarlo, Beatriz (1995), *Borges, un escritor en las orillas*, Buenos Aires: Ariel.
Sarlo, Beatriz (1998), *La máquina cultural: maestras, traductores y vanguardistas*, Buenos Aires: Ariel.
Sarmiento, Domingo Faustino (1962), *Recuerdos de provincia, precedido de Mi defensa*, Buenos Aires: Sur.
Sarmiento, Domingo Faustino (1977), in Nora Dottori and Silvia Zanetti (eds.), *Facundo: o, civilización y barbarie*, Caracas: Biblioteca Ayacucho.
Sarmiento, Domingo Faustino (2003), *Facundo: Civilization and Barbarism*, trans. Kathleen Ross, Berkeley, CA: University of California Press.
Sayers Peden, Margaret (1989), "Building a Translation, the Reconstruction Business: Poem 145 of Sor Juana Inés de la Cruz" in Ranier Schulte and John Biguenet (eds.), *The Craft of Translation*, Chicago, IL: University of Chicago Press, 13–27.
Scheiner, Corinne (2005), "Teleiopoiesis, Telepoesis, and the Practice of Comparative Literature" in *Comparative Literature* 57 (3): 239–45.
Schleiermacher, Friedrich (2012), "On the Different Methods of Translating," trans. Susan Bernofsky, in Lawrence Venuti (ed.), *The Translation Studies Reader*, New York: Routledge, 43–63.
Schulte, Ranier and John Biguenet (eds.) (1992), *Theories of Translation*, Chicago, IL: University of Chicago Press.
Schulte, Ranier (1997), "Prólogo" in Márgara Averbach and Lisa Bradford (eds.), *Traducción como cultura*, Rosario, Argentina: Beatriz Viterbo Editora, 9–12.
Schwarz, Roberto (1981), *Ao vencedor as batatas: forma literária e processo social nos inícios do romance brasileiro*, São Paulo: Livraria Duas Cidades.
Scliar, Moacyr (1995), *Contos reunidos*, São Paulo: Companhia das Letras.
Segato, Rita (2010), "Territory, Sovereignty, and Crimes of the Second State: The Writing on the Body of Murdered Women," trans. Sara Koopman, in Rosa-Linda Fregosa and Cynthia Bejarano (eds.), *Terrorizing Women: Feminicide in the Americas*, Durham, NC: Duke University Press.
Serres, Michel (2007), *The Parasite*, trans. Lawrence Schehr, Minneapolis, MN: University of Minnesota Press.
Shakespeare, William (1987), *A Midsummer Night's Dream*, approx. 1596, New York: Penguin Books.
Shumway, Nicolas (1991), *The Invention of Argentina*, Berkeley, CA: University of California Press.
Simon, Sherry (1996), *Gender in Translation: Cultural Identity and the Politics of Transmission*, London: Routledge.

Simon, Sherry (1999), "Translating and Interlingual Creation in the Contact Zone: Borderwriting in Quebec" in Susan Bassnett and Harish Trivedi (eds.), *Post-colonial Translation: Theory and Practice*, London: Routledge, 58–74.
Siskind, Mariano (2007), *Historia del Abasto*, Rosario, Argentina: Beatriz Viterbo Editora.
Siskind, Mariano (2010), "The Globalization of the Novel and the Novelization of the Global: A Critique of World Literature" in *Comparative Literature* 62 (4): 336–60.
Snell-Hornby, Mary (2006), *Turns of Translation Studies: New Paradigms or Shifting Viewpoints?* Amsterdam: John Benjamins Publishing Company.
Sommer, Doris (1991), *Foundational Fictions: The National Romances of Latin America*, Berkeley, CA: University of California Press.
Sorensen, Diana (1996), *Facundo and the Construction of Argentine Culture*, Austin, TX: University of Texas Press.
Speranza, Graciela (2006), *Fuera de campo: literatura y arte argentinos después de Duchamp*, Barcelona: Editorial Anagrama.
Spivak, Gayatri Chakravorty (2003), *Death of a Discipline*, New York: Columbia University Press.
Spivak, Gayatri Chakravorty (2005), "Translating into English" in Sandra Bermann and Michael Wood (eds.), *Nation, Language, and the Ethics of Translation*, Princeton, NJ: Princeton University Press, 93–110.
Spivak, Gayatri Chakravorty (2012), *An Aesthetic Education in the Era of Globalization*, Cambridge, MA: Harvard University Press.
St-Pierre, Paul and Prafulla C. Kar (eds.) (2005), *In Translation: Reflections, Refractions, Transformations*, Amsterdam: John Benjamins Publishing Company.
Stavans, Ilan (1996), *Julio Cortázar: A Study of the Short Fiction*, New York: Twayne Publishers.
Steiner, George (1975), *After Babel*, Oxford: Oxford University Press.
Stewart, Jon (1995), "Borges on Language and Translation" in *Philosophy and Literature* 19 (2): 320–9.
Tanselle, G. Thomas (1998), "The Footnote Demarginalized" in *Raritan* 18 (2): 137–45.
Thiem, Jon (1995), "The Translator as Hero in Postmodern Fiction" in *Translation and Literature* 4 (2): 207–18.
Thomas, Hugh (1993), *Conquest: Montezuma, Cortés, and the Fall of Old Mexico*, New York: Simon & Schuster.

Townsend, Camilla (2006), *Malintzin's Choices*, Albuquerque: University of New Mexico Press.

Translation Database, https://www.publishersweekly.com/pw/translation/home/index.html (last accessed June 12, 2020).

Tsurumi, Rebecca Riger (2012), *The Closed Hand: Images of the Japanese in Modern Peruvian Literature*, West Lafayette, IN: Purdue University Press.

Tymoczko, Maria and Edwin Gentzler (eds.) (2002), *Translation and Power*, Amherst, MA: University of Massachusetts Press.

Ulaby, Neda (2016), "*Arrival* Author's Approach to Science Fiction? Slow, Steady, and Successful" on *NPR*, at: www.npr.org/2016/11/11/501202681/arrival-authors-approach-to-science-fiction-slow-steady-and-successful (last accessed July 29, 2019).

Valencia, Sayak (2018), *Gore Capitalism*, trans. John Pluecker, Los Angeles, CA: Semiotext(e).

Vargas Llosa, Mario (2006), *Travesuras de la niña mala*, Madrid: Alfaguara.

Vargas Llosa, Mario (2008), *The Bad Girl*, trans. Edith Grossman, New York: Picador.

Venuti, Lawrence (ed.) (1992), *Rethinking Translation: Discourse, Subjectivity, Ideology*, London: Routledge.

Venuti, Lawrence (1995), *The Translator's Invisibility: A History of Translation*, London: Routledge.

Venuti, Lawrence (1996), "Translation and the Pedagogy of Literature" in *College English* 58 (3): 327–44.

Venuti, Lawrence (1998), *Scandals of Translation: Towards an Ethics of Difference*, London: Routledge.

Venuti, Lawrence (ed.) (2000), *The Translation Studies Reader*, London: Routledge.

Venuti, Lawrence (2013), "How to Read a Translation" [2004] in *Translation Changes Everything*, New York: Routledge.

Venuti, Lawrence (2019), *Contra Instrumentalism: a translation polemic*, Lincoln, NE: University of Nebraska Press.

Verissimo, Luis Fernando (2000), *Borges e os orangotangos eternos*, São Paulo, Brazil: Companhia das Letras.

Verissimo, Luis Fernando (2004), *Borges and the Eternal Orangutans*, trans. Margaret Jull Costa, New York: New Directions.

Vesna, Victoria (2007), "Introduction" in Victoria Vesna (ed.), *Database Aesthetics: Art in the Age of Information Overflow*, Minneapolis, MN: University of Minnesota Press, ix–xx.

Voigt, Rob and Dan Jurafsky (2012), "Towards a Literary Machine Translation: The Role of Referential Cohesion" at: http://www.stanford.edu/~jurafsky/voigtjurafsky12.pdf (last accessed June 10, 2020).

Waisman, Sergio (2001), "Ethics and Aesthetics North and South: Translation in the Work of Ricardo Piglia," in *Modern Language Quarterly: A Journal of Literary History* 62 (3): 259–83.

Waisman, Sergio (2003), "The Thousand and One Nights in Argentina: Translation, Narrative, and Politics in Borges, Puig, and Piglia," in *Comparative Literature Studies* 40 (4): 351–71.

Waisman, Sergio (2005), *Borges and Translation: The Irreverence of the Periphery*, Lewisburg, PA: Bucknell University Press.

Wallace, Melissa (2002), "Writing the Wrongs of Literature: The Figure of the Feminist and Post-Colonialist Translator" in *The Journal of the Midwest Modern Language Association* 35 (2): 65–74.

Wallerstein, Immanuel (2004), *World-systems Analysis: An Introduction*, Durham, NC: Duke University Press.

Walsh, Rodolfo (1967), "Nota al pie" in *Un kilo de oro*, Buenos Aires: Editorial J. Alvarez.

Weber, Samuel (2008), *Benjamin's –abilities*, Cambridge, MA: Harvard University Press.

Weinberger, Eliot (2016), *Nineteen Ways of Looking at Wang Wei*, 1987, New York: New Directions.

White, Patricia S. (1991), "Black and White and Read All Over: A Meditation on Footnotes" in *Text: Transactions of the Society for Textual Scholarship* 5: 81–90.

Whorf, Benjamin Lee (1940), "Science and Linguistics," in *Technology Review* 42: 229–31, 247–8.

Whorf, Benjamin Lee (1956), *Language, Thought, and Reality: Selected Writings*, Cambridge, MA: MIT Press.

Wiener, Gabriela (2004), "Mario Bellatin: 'Es un placer ver mutar tu propia palabra'" in *Lateral: Revista de Cultura* 11 (114): 10.

Willson, Patricia (1997), "Traductores en Sur: teoría y práctica" in Márgara Averbach and Lisa Bradford (eds.),*Traducción como cultura*, Rosario, Argentina: Beatriz Viterbo Editora, 133–40.

Willson, Patricia (2004), *La constelación del sur: traductores y traducciones en la literatura argentina del siglo XX*, Buenos Aires: Siglo Veintiuno Editores.

Wittgenstein, Ludwig (2001), *Tractatus Logico-Philosophicus*, 1921, trans. D. F. Pears and B. F. McGuinness, New York and London: Routledge.

Wood, Michael (2014), "What 'Justice' Means Around the World" at: https://www.huffpost.com/entry/justice-meaning_b_5161369 (last accessed June 11, 2020).

Wright, Lauren A. (2013), "Postscript: Writing After Conceptual Art" in *Frieze: Contemporary Art and Culture* 154: 170.

Yúdice, George, Juan Flores, and Jean Franco (eds.) (1992), *On Edge: The Crisis of Contemporary Latin American Culture*, Minneapolis, MN: University of Minnesota Press.

Zaid, Gabriel (2005), "Nota al pie de las notas al pie" in *Letras Libres* 7 (74): 44–5.

Zimmer, Zac (2013), "A Year in Rewind, and Five Centuries of Continuity: *El año del desierto*'s Dialectical Image" in *MLN* 128 (2): 373–83.

Index

Aira, César 13, 42, 47 n.19, 49
   El congreso de literatura 13, 19, 42–52
   La princesa primavera 13, 20, 42, 136–40, 142
Allen, Esther 6 n.8, 8 n.10, 152
Andrade, Oswald de 4–5
anti-neocolonialism 4, 11–12, 21, 84 n.25, 141, 154
Apter, Emily 18, 40–1, 57–8
Arrival (film) 55–6
Arrojo, Rosemary 18, 25, 27 n.5, 95 n.9, 107, 125 n.6
author sign 32, 38, 40, 43 n.18, 52, 88–90, 108–10, 128, 138–9
authorship 2, 10, 15, 23–6, 30, 32–6, 39, 93, 110, 138–9, 149, 156 *see also* privileged original

Bellatin, Mario 13–14, 87–92, 115–18, 151
   El jardín de la señora Murakami 19–20, 92–3, 101–15, 118–19
Benesdra, Salvador, *El traductor* 19–20, 66, 70–4, 76, 82–3, 84, 140–2
Benjamin, Walter 19, 64–6, 68
   language forest, 77, 79, 86, 146 n.23
Bhabha, Homi 19, 147–9
Borges and the Eternal Orangutans see Verissimo, Luis Fernando
Borges, Jorge Luis 8–11, 19, 28 n.9, 37–8, 56, 118, 125–8, 132–3, 148 *see also* Pierre Menard; as fictional character, 35–40

Campos, Augusto de 5–6
Campos, Haroldo de 5–6, 28, 49
cannibalism 4–6
Casanova, Pascale 129–32, 143

Cassin, Barbara 19, 57, 58 n.4
Catford, J. C. 56 n.2, 76 n.20
center/periphery 2, 10–12, 16, 19, 29, 71, 93, 97, 111, 129–34, 136–41, 142, 148–9
Chamberlain, Lori 18, 23, 36, 46, 58, 82 n.24
Choi, Don Mee 11 n.16, 84 n.25, 154
cloning 1, 18, 40–53
   Adam and Eve 45–6
cognates 19, 59, 70–6, 78–80, 82–4
Cortázar, Julio 12, 24–7, 29
Cronin, Michael 74–6
cultural geopolitics 2, 11–17, 20–1, 29, 40–1, 52–3, 71–3, 101, 129–33, 131, 141, 148–9

de Man, Paul 65, 66 n.10, 77 n.21
De Santis, Pablo, *La traducción* 19–20, 66–70, 83, 134–6, 142
Deleuze, Gilles and Félix Guattari 51–2, 57
denaturalization 16, 57, 61, 63 n.8, 90, 101–2, 127
Derrida, Jacques, 19, 55, 59–61, 67 n.11, 82–85, 93–4, 114
   as fictional character, 1, 75–6
deviation 41, 46–8, 52, 143 *see also* infidelity
discursive power 2, 5, 11, 15, 34, 36, 38–40, 52, 60, 71, 89, 93–5, 99–100, 102–4, 140, 148–9
distancing reading, 19, 21, 59, 70, 73–4, 74 n.17, 84–6, 151
   distinction from distant reading, 85
domestication/foreignization 27 n.6, 73–4, 74 n.17

Faces in the Crowd see Luiselli, Valeria
Feierstein, Liliana 17, 87, 94–5, 114

fictional turn 17, 21
fidelity see infidelity
footnotes 19, 60 n.6, 93–100, 103–15
 relation to photography, 91–2

Glantz, Margo 4 n.4, 88
global publishing industry 12, 15, 17, 71, 121, 134 n.16, 141, 148
globalization 1, 14–15, 20, 57, 61, 70, 73–4, 87 n.1, 115, 136

hermeneutics
 and detective work 36–8, 62, 66, 69–70, 99–100, 143
 hermeneutic instability 37–9, 46, 80, 94–5, 100, 104, 107–8, 110, 113–15
Humboldt, Wilhelm von 56

identity 14, 32, 41, 46–8, 50, 61, 66, 69, 89, 108, 138, 147
ideology 3–4, 11–12, 16, 28 n.9, 74, 131, 139–41, 152
infidelity 9, 23–4, 36, 40, 46, 48, 52, 138–9
intellectual influence 19, 24, 28–9, 35, 38–40, 42–3, 51–3, 90, 153
intellectual property 2, 10, 14–15, 19, 24, 27, 59, 87–8, 93, 116, 128, 149, 151, 153–6
intersemiotic translation 37 n.13
intertextuality 29, 32–5, 37–8, 43, 124 n.4, 144
iteration 9, 15, 42, 46, 51, 58, 61, 64, 70, 77, 98, 126, 148–9, 151

Jacobs, Carol 65

Kawabata, Yasunari 101, 108–9, 113, 151
kinship
 among languages, 70, 80
 patrilinear, 19, 23–4, 27–8, 31–2, 38–9, 153

Laddaga, Reinaldo 49–50
Latin American literature
 Boom, the 12–13, 18
 fictions of translation in 1–2, 12–14, 18
 Japanese literature in 29–34, 87, 90, 100–2 see also Bellatin and Kawabata
 tradition of translation in 2–14
Levine, Suzanne Jill 13, 16 n.18, 143
Lezra, Jacques 15, 57 n.3, 60 n.6, 78–9
linguistic incommensurability 55–7, 64, 68, 83–4 see also untranslatability
literary conference 36–7, 41–53, 66, 88, 134–5
Literary Conference, The see Aira, César
literary consecration 12, 15, 38, 52–3, 131
literary forgery 1, 18, 30–2, 40, 87–92, 115, 121–2, 139 see also Bellatin, Mario
Luiselli, Valeria, Los ingrávidos 20, 121–7, 134

Malintzin (La Malinche) 2–4
monstrosity 3, 23–4, 29, 35–6, 40–1, 44, 48, 52
Mounin, Georges 59, 61
Mrs. Murakami's Garden see Bellatin, Mario

neoliberalism 1, 11 n.16, 42, 71, 87 n.1, 134–5, 140, 145

Oedipal violence 28–9, 37–9

parasite 94, 113–14
Past, The see Pauls, Alan
Pauls, Alan
 Historia del pelo 14, 75 n.19, 78–9
 on Mario Bellatin 89, 91, 108
 El pasado 14, 19, 70, 74–83

Paz, Octavio 4 n.4, 64
Pierre Menard, 8–10, 111, 118, 125–8, 133 n.15, 148 *see also* Borges, Jorge Luis
Piglia, Ricardo 6–8
Pires Vieira, Else Ribeiro 12, 17
planetarity 70, 85–6 *see also* Spivak, Gayatri Chakravorty
Poe, Edgar Allan 24, 35–6, 37 n.12, 39
Ponce, Néstor 13, 66
privileged original 4, 9, 15, 23–9, 36, 38–41, 44–5, 48–53, 64–9, 92–4, 94 n.6, 97–8, 103, 107–8, 112, 115, 123, 148–9, 153

rhizome *see* Deleuze and Guattari
Rivera Garza, Cristina, *El mal de la taiga* 20, 143–9

Saer, Juan José 62–3, 70, 77
Safranchik, Graciela, *El cangrejo* 18, 29–34, 52
Santiago, Silviano 11, 121, 127 n.9, 148 n.24
Sapir, Edward and Benjamin Whorf 56
Sarmiento, Domingo Faustino 6–8
Schleiermacher, Friedrich 27–8, 35
Scliar, Moacyr 18, 97–9, 107
Serres, Michel 80, 114
Shakespeare, William 5, 42, 78–80, 155
Shook, David 14, 90, 116–19
Siskind, Mariano 13, 122 n.1
Spivak, Gayatri Chakravorty 70, 73, 82 n.24, 85, 154–5
Steiner, George 23, 56 n.2

Taiga Syndrome, The see Rivera Garza, Cristina
teleopoiesis 85, 156

Tower of Babel 67–9, 137 n.19
transcreation 5, 41, 49, 152, 155
translation
 as cause of death 1, 36–7, 62, 67–9, 77 n.21, 97–100, 134 *see also* Oedipal violence
 as creative act 15, 19, 24, 27, 41, 48, 96, 107, 140, 155
 as derivative, *see* privileged original
 equivalence (general) and economics 59–61, 63, 69, 77, 80, 82, 131
 gendered metaphors 18, 23–8, 30–4, 39–40
 as intellectual labor 15, 20, 140
 material conditions 2, 15–16, 21, 42, 71–3, 137–9, 140, 145, 153
 as metonymy 66, 77, 82, 85 n.26
 and pedagogy 20, 151–6
 reciprocal creation 2, 52–3, 127, 148
 situatedness 16–21, 47, 56–8, 61, 65, 70, 74 n.17, 76–7, 115, 127 n.9, 139, 143, 156
 spatial metaphors 20, 25, 48, 96–100, 122–49 *see also* Benjamin: language forest
 untranslatability 18, 42, 55–86, 110

Venuti, Lawrence 16, 27 n.6, 73–4, 139, 151 n.1, 152
Verissimo, Luis Fernando, *Borges e os orangotangos eternos* 18, 35–40, 66

Walsh, Rodolfo 18, 96–7, 99–100
Weinberger, Eliot 155
Wittgenstein, Ludwig 56
Wood, Michael 57 n.3, 76

Zohn, Harry 65, 84 n.25

www.ingramcontent.com/pod-product-compliance
Lightning Source LLC
Chambersburg PA
CBHW070831300426
44111CB00014B/2519